Better Homes and Gardens®

ENCYCLOPEDIA
of
COOKING

Volume 14

A tender, flaky lattice pastry and the winning filling combination of sliced, fresh rhubarb and canned tart red cherries make up rosy Cherry-Rhubarb Pie (see page 1676 for recipe).

On the cover: If ever there was a Perfect Apple Pie, this is it. Nicely spiced with cinnamon and nutmeg, this fruit-filled beauty is decked out with cornucopias of good, nippy cheese.

BETTER HOMES AND GARDENS BOOKS
NEW YORK • DES MOINES

PIE

Special hints on how to combine crust and filling for meat, vegetable, and dessert pies.

Pies of one kind or another have been enjoyed for centuries. The English lay claim to the first pie but, like many other dishes, just when and where savory and sweet fillings were first served with a crust of pastry has never been pinpointed.

Today, the cuisine of almost every country contains pie of some sort, but pies are probably most commonly associated with English and United States cooking. The people of both of these countries enjoy a variety of pies. Meat pies are especially popular in England, while dessert pies hold the premier position with most people in the United States.

As far back as the fourteenth century, pie shops in London were doing a thriving business selling pies filled with meat, fish, or poultry and, according to one nursery rhyme, even with live blackbirds. During the mid-1700s, numerous piemen made their living by roaming England's countryside selling their wares. The popularity of this profession began to fall off when people became aware of food spoilage. This was especially so in Victorian times. Piemen were still prevalent in the early 1900s but, today, pie manufacturers who make and sell huge quantites of pies daily have virtually eliminated the need for the quaint pieman and his product.

Over the last several centuries, mince pie has become traditional at English Christmas dinners. Sometimes designated as Christmas pie, mince pie was originally a huge pie filled with a mixture of ox tongue, poultry, fruits, and spices. The mince pie of today, however, differs from the first mince pie in both size and ingredients. Present-day English cooks make tiny pies out of mincemeat made of suet, dried fruit, and spices.

The love of pies and pie baking was one of the things that the Pilgrims brought with them from England. Besides meat pies, both pumpkin and cranberry pies are mentioned as being part of the fare of these early settlers.

Like the English pies, the pies made by these colonists were usually deep pies. However, during the eighteenth century, the preference of Americans turned to shallow pies, which sometimes had more crust than filling. This development is often attributed, probably rightly so, to thriftiness because by making shallow pies, the housewife could stretch precious ingredients over several meals.

As is evidenced by the saying, "as American as apple pie," very few other foods are considered as traditionally American. Even though apple pie is not an American invention, it is so widely enjoyed that it is permanently linked with the cuisine of the United States. Due to its popularity, variations as simple as the addition of a piece of cheese or as different as a custard-apple pie, apple-raisin pie, and sour cream-apple pie have been developed over the years.

During the 1800s, housewives used fresh apples while they were in season, then dried apples during the rest of the year. Today, canned or frozen apples have replaced the dried apples of yesteryear. Although in most parts of the country apple pie is reserved as dessert for dinner or supper, it is traditionally eaten for breakfast in New England. When one visitor questioned this custom, Emerson summed up the attitude that pie is a logical breakfast food in his reply, "What is pie for?"

Types of pies

Almost anything can be used as a pie filling. In fact, many cooks find that they can often improve leftovers by adding a

Plump, fresh blueberries generously fill this Lemon-Crusted Blueberry Pie. Fresh lemon juice and peel in both the pie filling and the pastry subtly complement the juicy berries.

few ingredients and baking them in a piecrust. Even though so many combinations of ingredients can be used as pie fillings, pies can be divided into three types—meat, vegetable, and dessert pies.

Meat pies: Centuries ago, homemakers found that a savory meat, poultry, or fish mixture combined with a pastry or a biscuit crust was a hearty and delicious main dish. Like many dishes, meat pie recipes survived the years and are still popular. Generally, the meat is finely chopped or ground, but some meat pies such as the English favorite, steak-and-kidney pie, contain larger pieces of meat. Onions and other vegetables are frequently ingredients in the well-seasoned meat pie fillings.

Pork or Beef Pie

In saucepan cook $\frac{1}{2}$ cup chopped onion in 6 tablespoons butter or margarine till tender. Blend in $\frac{1}{2}$ cup all-purpose flour and 1 teaspoon salt. Dissolve 3 beef bouillon cubes in 3 cups boiling water. Stir into flour mixture all at once; cook and stir till thickened and bubbly. Add 3 cups cubed cooked pork *or* beef; one 10-ounce package frozen peas and carrots, cooked and drained; and $\frac{1}{4}$ cup parsley. Heat through. Pour meat mixture into 2-quart casserole.

Meanwhile, prepare pastry for 1-crust 9-inch pie (See *Pastry*); roll $\frac{1}{2}$ to 1 inch larger than top of casserole. Place pastry atop *hot* meat mixture. Cut slits in top. Turn under edge and flute. Brush with milk. Bake at 450° for 20 to 25 minutes. Makes 6 to 8 servings.

Vegetable pies: Although not as well known as the other two types of pies, vegetable pies are equally delicious. Usually one-crust pies filled with a vegetable-custard mixture, vegetable pies can be served as an appetizer, as a main dish accompaniment, or even as the main dish at a brunch or at a light, later-evening meal.

French Onion Pie

Serve in tiny wedges as an appetizer or in larger pieces as a meat accompaniment—

    Pastry for 1–crust 9-inch pie
      (See *Pastry*)
1 **3½-ounce can French fried**
      onions (2 cups)
      • • •
4 **eggs**
2 **cups milk**
2 **ounces sharp process American**
      cheese, shredded (½ cup)
½ **teaspoon salt**
      Dash cayenne
4 **ounces sharp process American**
      cheese, shredded (1 cup)

Prepare pastry for 9-inch pie. Line pie plate; flute edges. Bake piecrust at 450° till golden, about 7 to 8 minutes. Remove piecrust from oven. Reduce oven temperature to 325°. While pastry is still warm, fill bottom with *1½ cups* of the French fried onions. (Reserve remaining ½ cup onions for garnish.) Beat eggs slightly; blend in milk, the ½ cup shredded cheese, the salt, and cayenne. Pour this mixture over onions in pastry shell. Sprinkle the 1 cup shredded cheese over pie. Bake at 325° for 45 minutes. Sprinkle reserved onions around the edge of pie. Bake till a knife inserted just off-center comes out clean, about 5 to 10 minutes more. Let the pie stand at room temperature 10 minutes before serving. Makes 6 servings.

Dessert pies: Fluffy chiffon pies, meringue-topped cream pies, luscious fruit pies, and rich custard pies are all included in the most popular type, the dessert pie. Although all are sweet pies, dessert pies can be further divided into one-crust pies, two-crust pies, and deep-dish pies.

Most one-crust pies are made in two steps —baking the crust, and making the filling. When making pastry for a one-crust pie, prevent large air bubbles from forming in the crust by pricking with a fork before baking. To reduce shrinkage, shape the pastry in the pan without stretching it.

The filling for a one-crust pie may be a cooked pudding-type mixture, or it may be an uncooked mixture. Although the filling is usually made separately and poured into the baked pastry shell, a few types of one-crust pies, for example custard, pumpkin, and pecan pies, are made by baking the filling and the crust together. In this type of pie, holes in the crust or an oven temperature that is too low can cause the pie to have a soggy crust.

Quite frequently, one-crust pies are completed with a fluffy meringue. For a meringue-topped pie, swirl or pipe the meringue onto the filling (do this when the filling is warm if it is a cream filling), then bake the pie until the meringue is golden brown. Whipped cream is another common topping for one-crust pies.

Pumpkin-Pecan Pie

Two favorites, pumpkin and pecans, in one pie—

3 **slightly beaten eggs**
1 **cup canned or mashed cooked**
      pumpkin
1 **cup sugar**
½ **cup dark corn syrup**
1 **teaspoon vanilla**
½ **teaspoon ground cinnamon**
¼ **teaspoon salt**
1 ***unbaked* 9-inch pastry shell**
      (See *Pastry*)
      • • •
1 **cup chopped pecans**
      Whipped cream

In small mixing bowl combine slightly beaten eggs, pumpkin, sugar, dark corn syrup, vanilla, ground cinnamon, and salt; mix thoroughly. Pour into unbaked pastry shell. Top with pecans. Bake at 350° till knife inserted halfway between center and edge comes out clean, about 40 minutes. Chill thoroughly; serve topped with a dollop of whipped cream.

Berry Cheesecake Pie

1 10¾- or 11-ounce package
  cheesecake mix
⅓ cup chopped almonds, toasted
1 *baked* 9-inch pastry shell,
  cooled (See *Pastry*)
1 cup sugar
2 tablespoons cornstarch
1 quart fresh strawberries
1 3-ounce package strawberry-
  flavored gelatin
1 tablespoon butter or margarine
1 tablespoon lemon juice

Prepare cheesecake mix following package directions; stir in nuts. Pour into pastry shell; chill 1 hour. In saucepan combine sugar and cornstarch. Mash *1 cup* berries; add water to make 2 cups. Stir into sugar mixture. Cook and stir till thick and bubbly; cook 1 minute more. Strain. Add gelatin, butter, and lemon juice; stir till gelatin dissolves. Chill till partially set. Spoon *1½ cups* of the gelatin mixture over cheesecake. Slice remaining berries; arrange over pie. Spoon remaining gelatin mixture over berries. Chill till set.

Dreamy-High Pumpkin Pie

1 cup sugar
1 envelope unflavored gelatin
1 teaspoon ground cinnamon
¼ teaspoon ground nutmeg
3 slightly beaten egg yolks
¾ cup milk
1 cup cooked or canned pumpkin
3 egg whites
  Graham Cracker Crust
  (See *Crumb Crust*)
  Whipped cream
½ cup flaked coconut

In saucepan mix ⅔ *cup* sugar, gelatin, cinnamon, ½ teaspoon salt, and nutmeg. Combine egg yolks and milk; add to gelatin mixture. Cook and stir till slightly thickened. Stir in pumpkin. Chill till mixture mounds slightly, stirring often. Beat egg whites till soft peaks form. Gradually add remaining sugar, beating to stiff peaks. Fold pumpkin mixture into whites. Pile into Graham Cracker Crust. Chill till firm. Top with whipped cream and coconut.

Buttermint Chiffon Pie

1½ cups crushed chocolate wafers
½ cup sifted confectioners' sugar
6 tablespoons butter or margarine,
  melted
24 buttermints, crushed (½ cup)
1 envelope unflavored gelatin
1¼ cups milk
3 beaten egg yolks
  Green food coloring
½ cup whipping cream
3 egg whites
¼ cup granulated sugar

Combine wafer crumbs, confectioners' sugar, and butter. Press into 9-inch pie plate; chill. In saucepan combine mints and gelatin; gradually stir in milk and egg yolks. Cook and stir over medium-low heat till slightly thickened, 10 to 12 minutes. Stir in a few drops food coloring; cool. Whip cream till soft peaks form. Beat egg whites till soft peaks form; gradually add granulated sugar, beating to stiff peaks. Fold egg yolk mixture, then whipped cream into egg whites. Spoon into pie shell; chill till firm, about 5 hours. Garnish with additional whipped cream, if desired.

Pear Chiffon Pie

1 29-ounce can pear halves
⅔ cup sugar
1 envelope unflavored gelatin
3 slightly beaten egg yolks
¼ teaspoon grated lemon peel
1 tablespoon lemon juice
3 egg whites
1 *baked* 9-inch pastry shell,
  cooled (See *Pastry*)
  Whipped cream

Drain pears, reserving ¼ cup syrup and 1 pear half. With fork, mash remaining pears; drain. Combine ⅓ *cup* sugar, gelatin, and ¼ teaspoon salt; stir in reserved syrup, egg yolks, lemon peel, and lemon juice. Cook and stir till slightly thickened. Add mashed pears. Cool till mixture mounds. Beat egg whites to soft peaks; gradually add remaining ⅓ cup sugar, beating to stiff peaks. Fold in pear mixture. Turn into baked pastry; chill. Garnish with whipped cream and reserved pear half, sliced.

Strawberry-Mallow Pie

    3½ cups miniature marshmallows
    ¾ cup milk
    1 cup whipping cream
    ½ teaspoon vanilla
    1 *baked* 9-inch pastry shell,
        cooled (See *Pastry*)
    1 21-ounce can strawberry pie
        filling

Set aside ½ cup marshmallows; melt remaining marshmallows with milk over low heat, stirring constantly. Chill, without stirring, till partially set. Whip cream. Fold cream, vanilla, and dash salt into marshmallow mixture.

Spoon *half* the mixture into pastry shell. Cover with pie filling, reserving ½ cup. Fold reserved marshmallows into remaining cream mixture; spread over strawberry layer. Garnish with reserved filling. Chill thoroughly.

Fruit is the most frequent filling for two-crust pies. Fresh apples, blueberries, rhubarb, cherries, peaches, apricots, and many other fruits are particularly tasty when mixed with sugar, seasonings, and a little thickening agent and then baked between two tender, flaky layers of pastry. Canned and dried fruit also make delicious pies. As with one-crust pies, prevent a soggy bottom crust by having the oven at the correct temperature and by making sure there are no holes in the bottom piecrust. It is also important to make sure that the pie bakes long enough.

Apple-Apricot Pie

Combine ⅓ cup granulated sugar, ⅓ cup brown sugar, 3 tablespoons all-purpose flour, ¼ teaspoon salt, and ¼ teaspoon ground cinnamon; stir into one 20-ounce can pie-sliced apples, undrained. Add 1 tablespoon lemon juice and mix well. Drain one 30-ounce can apricot halves. Cut apricot halves in half; fold into apples.

Prepare pastry for 2-crust 9-inch pie (See *Pastry*). Line 9-inch pie plate with pastry; add fruit mixture. Dot with 1 tablespoon butter. Adjust top crust, cutting steam vents; seal and flute. Sprinkle top with additional granulated sugar. Bake at 400° for 40 minutes.

Deep-dish pies are actually one-crust pies with the pastry on top of rather than under the filling. These pies are called deep-dish because they are made in a deep-dish pie plate or a shallow casserole. Deep-dish apple, the most common pie of this type, is a particular favorite in certain parts of the United States such as in New England. This type of pie, which is especially delectable warm, is served in spoonfuls rather than wedges and often is accompanied by cream.

Deep-Dish Apple Pie

Serve warm with light cream—

    10 cups thinly sliced, peeled
         apples (about 8 apples)
     1 cup sugar
     1 tablespoon all-purpose flour
     ½ teaspoon ground cinnamon
     ¼ teaspoon ground nutmeg
     ¼ teaspoon salt
     3 tablespoons butter or margarine
              • • •
     1 cup sifted all-purpose flour
     ⅛ teaspoon salt
     ⅓ cup shortening
     2 to 3 tablespoons cold milk
        Milk
        Sugar
        Light cream

Place thinly sliced apples in an 11¾x7½x1¾-inch baking dish. In mixing bowl combine sugar, the 1 tablespoon all-purpose flour, ground cinnamon, ground nutmeg, and the ¼ teaspoon salt; sprinkle over apples, mixing lightly. Dot with butter or margarine.

For pastry, in mixing bowl sift together the 1 cup all-purpose flour and the ⅛ teaspoon salt; cut in shortening till mixture resembles coarse crumbs. Add milk gradually, tossing with fork till flour-shortening mixture is just dampened. Shape into ball.

On lightly floured surface, roll dough to 12¾x8½-inch rectangle, ⅛ inch thick. Place crust over apples; flute edges. Brush crust with additional milk; cut slits for escape of steam. Sprinkle crust with a little sugar. Bake at 400° till done, about 45 to 50 minutes. Serve warm with light cream.

Preparation and storage

A pie is made up of two distinct parts, the crust and the filling. In order to win compliments on your pies, you must master the art of combining a tender, flaky piecrust and a succulent filling. Although this may sound difficult, practice and diligence will assuredly pay off with delectable pies that will delight any guest.

Crust: The crust of a pie provides a shell or foundation to hold the soft filling. This piecrust is most commonly made of pastry. No matter whether you make the pastry from the basic ingredients or from a packaged piecrust mix, be sure to handle it gently and avoid overmixing (see *Pastry*). The individual recipe will specify whether or not the pastry should be baked before the filling is added.

Although a pastry crust is most popular, some one-crust pies have other kinds of crusts, such as a crust made from graham cracker crumbs, cookie crumbs, or coconut (see *Crumb Crust, Crust* for additional information). Unlike pastry, which is rolled out, these crusts are molded to shape by firmly pressing them into the pie plate. The crust is then baked or chilled before the filling is added.

Filling: Although pie fillings are many and varied, they can be generally divided into two categories—cooked and uncooked. Cooked fillings are either cooked before they are put in the pastry, such as the canned fillings, or are baked with the pastry. Uncooked fillings include those that do not need any cooking or baking. At least one kind of pie—Alaska pie—doesn't fit into either category exactly. However, since it requires baking for a brief period of time to brown the meringue, Alaska pie is grouped with the cooked fillings.

Meat, vegetable, custard, and some types of fruit, cream, and Alaska pies have cooked fillings. Although there may be some variance, as a general rule, meat and cream fillings are at least partially cooked before they are spooned into the piecrust. The other cooked fillings are put into an unbaked piecrust uncooked and then undergo cooking as the pie is baked.

Pie cues

Good equipment makes any job easier. For pies, a well-equipped cook needs a pastry blender, a rolling pin with stockinette, and a pastry cloth. A pastry wheel is also handy.

To prevent burning, protect the edge of the pastry with an aluminum foil collar during part of the baking. Fold a 2½-inch strip of foil around the rim, making sure that the foil covers all the fluted edge.

Before cutting a meringue-topped pie, dip the knife in water. (No need to dry it off.) Repeat whenever meringue sticks.

For a nonstick crumb crust, wrap a hot, wet towel under the bottom and around the sides of the pie plate just before serving the pie. Hold the towel against the plate for a few minutes. This loosens the crust so that each piece of pie slips out easily.

Spruce up a pie by decorating it with pastry cutouts. Cut the pastry with small cookie or hors d'oeuvre cutters, or make your own pattern and cut around it. Arrange the cutouts on the pie before baking, or bake them separately and then place them on the filling.

Glaze the top crust of two-crust pies to make them look extra special. Try brushing the unbaked crust with water or butter and then sprinkle it lightly with sugar, or brush the crust lightly with beaten egg. A light coating of milk also gives the top crust a pretty finish.

Spicy Pumpkin-Cheese Pie

Cream cheese adds smoothness—

Beat together one 8-ounce package cream cheese, softened; ¾ cup brown sugar; 1 teaspoon ground cinnamon; 1 teaspoon ground nutmeg; ½ teaspoon ground ginger; and ½ teaspoon salt. Add 3 eggs, one at a time; beat well after each. Stir in 1 cup canned or mashed cooked pumpkin, 1 cup milk, and 1 teaspoon vanilla. Pour into one *unbaked* 9-inch pastry shell. (See *Pastry*.)

Bake at 375° till knife inserted halfway between center and edge comes out clean, about 45 to 50 minutes. Chill thoroughly. Garnish with whipped cream and ground nutmeg.

Vanilla Cream Pie

Also try chocolate and butterscotch variations—

In saucepan combine ¾ cup sugar, ⅓ cup all-purpose flour *or* 3 tablespoons cornstarch, and ¼ teaspoon salt. Gradually add 2 cups milk, mixing well. Cook and stir till the mixture is thickened and bubbly. Cook 2 minutes more. Remove from heat. Stir a small amount hot mixture into 3 slightly beaten egg yolks; immediately return to hot mixture. Cook and stir 2 minutes more. Remove from heat. Add 2 tablespoons butter and 1 teaspoon vanilla. Pour into one *baked* 9-inch pastry shell, cooled (See *Pastry*). Spread Meringue atop hot filling, sealing to edge of pastry. Bake at 350˚ for 12 to 15 minutes. Cool thoroughly.

Meringue: In mixing bowl beat 3 egg whites with ½ teaspoon vanilla and ¼ teaspoon cream of tartar till soft peaks form. Add 6 tablespoons sugar, beating till stiff peaks form.

Chocolate Cream Pie: Increase sugar to 1 cup in Vanilla Cream Pie. Chop two 1-ounce squares unsweetened chocolate; add with milk.

Butterscotch Pie: Substitute brown sugar for granulated sugar in Vanilla Cream Pie. Increase butter or margarine to 3 tablespoons.

Celebrate Washington's birthday or any special occasion by serving Cherry Tarts. Prepare the pastry and filling separately; then assemble tarts and decorate with pastry hatchets.

Layer the creamy marshmallow mixture and strawberry pie filling in a flaky pastry shell for delicious Strawberry-Mallow Pie.

Custard-Peach Pie

Combine one 21-ounce can peach pie filling and one 8¾-ounce can crushed pineapple, drained. Turn into one *baked* 9-inch pastry shell, cooled (See *Pastry*). In mixer bowl beat together 1 cup dairy sour cream and one 3-ounce package cream cheese, softened; add 2 slightly beaten eggs and ⅓ cup sugar, beating till smooth. Pour over peach mixture. Sprinkle a little ground nutmeg over top. Bake at 375° till filling is set, about 30 to 35 minutes.

Strawberry Alaska Pie

Soften 1 pint lemon sherbet and spread evenly in bottom of one *baked* 9-inch pastry shell, cooled (See *Pastry*). Freeze solidly, at least 4 to 5 hours or overnight.

Slice 1 quart fresh strawberries, sweeten with 1 tablespoon sugar. Prepare Meringue (see Vanilla Cream Pie, page 1673). Remove pie from freezer. Working quickly, arrange strawberries over sherbet. Spread Meringue over berries, being careful to seal to edge of pastry. Place pie on cutting board; bake at 475° till golden, about 5 to 6 minutes. Cut with sharp knife dipped in water, and serve immediately.

Citrus-Cheese Pie

Using package directions, prepare and bake 9-inch pastry shell from 1 stick precrust mix; cool. (Be sure to flute edges high.) Prepare one 3⅝-ounce package lemon pudding mix according to package directions for pie filling, *using 1 slightly beaten egg* in place of egg yolks called for; omit meringue. Stir 4 tablespoons butter or margarine into hot pie filling. Cover with waxed paper; cool.

Blend one 4-ounce package whipped cream cheese with 2 tablespoons sugar, 1 teaspoon shredded orange peel, and ½ teaspoon vanilla. Spread evenly in bottom of baked pastry shell; chill. Prepare one 3-ounce package orange-flavored gelatin according to package directions; cool till mixture begins to set.

Beat lemon pie filling till smooth; spread *evenly* over cream cheese layer in pastry shell. Top with *1 cup* of the orange gelatin. (Use remaining gelatin for salad or dessert.) Chill thoroughly. Prepare one 2-ounce package dessert topping mix according to package directions. Spoon whipped topping into center of pie; garnish with orange sections, if desired.

Lemon-Crusted Blueberry Pie

Prepare Lemon Pastry. In mixing bowl combine 4 cups blueberries, ¾ to 1 cup sugar, 3 tablespoons flour, ½ teaspoon grated lemon peel, and dash salt. Line a 9-inch pie plate with pastry; pour in filling. Drizzle with 1 to 2 teaspoons lemon juice and dot with 1 tablespoon butter. Adjust top crust; cut slits. Seal; flute. Bake at 400° for 35 to 40 minutes.

Lemon Pastry: Sift together 2 cups sifted all-purpose flour and 1 teaspoon salt; stir in ½ teaspoon grated lemon peel. Cut in ⅔ cup shortening with pastry blender or blending fork till pieces are size of small peas.

Mix together 4 to 6 tablespoons cold water and 1 tablespoon lemon juice. Sprinkle 1 tablespoon liquid over part of flour mixture. Toss with fork; push to side of bowl. Sprinkle next tablespoon liquid over dry portion. Mix lightly; push to moistened part at side of bowl. Repeat with remaining liquid till all flour mixture is moistened. Divide into two portions; form into balls. Flatten balls, one at a time, on lightly floured surface. Roll from center to edge to ⅛-inch thickness.

Cherry Tarts

1½ cups sifted all-purpose flour
1 teaspoon salt
½ cup shortening
4 or 5 tablespoons cold water
1 16-ounce can pitted tart red
   cherries (water pack)
¾ cup sugar
3 tablespoons cornstarch
1 tablespoon butter or margarine
¼ teaspoon red food coloring
4 or 5 drops almond extract

For tart shells sift together flour and ¾ teaspoon salt. With pastry blender cut in shortening till pieces are size of small peas. Sprinkle cold water, 1 tablespoon at a time, over flour-shortening mixture; toss well after each addition, till completely moistened.

Form pastry into ball; flatten ball slightly on lightly floured surface. Roll to ⅛-inch thickness. Cut into eight 5-inch circles. Fit circles over inverted custard cups, pressing out air bubbles. Prick bottom and sides of each shell with fork.

Cut "hatchets" from remaining pastry dough; place on cookie sheet. Bake tart shells and "hatchets" at 450° till golden, 10 to 12 minutes. ("Hatchets" will be done sooner, so watch them!) Cool slightly; remove from cups.

Meanwhile, to prepare filling, drain cherries, reserving ¾ cup juice. Combine sugar, cornstarch, and ¼ teaspoon salt; stir in reserved juice. Cook and stir over high heat till thickened and bubbly. Stir in butter, food coloring, almond extract, and drained cherries. Cool; spoon into baked tart shells. Top each tart with baked pastry "hatchet." Makes 8 tarts.

Sliced Pear Pie

Prepare pastry for 9-inch lattice-top pie (See *Pastry*). In mixing bowl toss together 5 fresh pears, peeled and sliced; ¾ to 1 cup sugar; ¼ cup all-purpose flour; ½ teaspoon ground cinnamon; dash salt; ½ teaspoon shredded lemon peel; and 2 tablespoons lemon juice. Arrange fruit mixture in pastry-lined 9-inch pie plate. Dot with 2 tablespoons butter or margarine. Adjust lattice top; seal and flute edge. Cover edge of pie with foil. Bake at 425° till done, about 35 minutes. Remove foil after 25 minutes.

European Apple Pie

½ cup whole wheat flour
1 cup sifted all-purpose flour
2 tablespoons sugar
   Dash salt
½ teaspoon baking powder
6 tablespoons butter or margarine
⅓ cup dairy sour cream
¼ cup graham cracker crumbs
6 medium apples, peeled and
   diced (about 5 cups)
1 8¾-ounce can apricot
   halves, drained
½ cup sugar
½ teaspoon ground cinnamon

In mixing bowl combine whole wheat flour, all-purpose flour, the 2 tablespoons sugar, dash salt, and baking powder; cut in butter or margarine. Stir in sour cream. Turn out on lightly floured board; knead a few strokes to form a ball. Divide dough in half; roll half to fit a 9-inch pie plate. Sprinkle graham cracker crumbs evenly in bottom of pie plate; fit pastry over crumbs. Arrange apples and apricots in crust. Combine the ½ cup sugar and the cinnamon; sprinkle over filling. Roll out remaining pastry for top crust; slash to allow steam to escape. Fit over filling; seal edges and flute. Bake at 350° for 20 minutes; reduce temperature to 300° and bake 40 minutes more.

Cocktail Chiffon Pie

In top of double boiler, soften 1 envelope unflavored gelatin in ½ cup cold water. Add 3 slightly beaten egg yolks and dash salt. Cook and stir over hot, not boiling water till gelatin dissolves and mixture thickens, about 7 minutes. Remove from heat; stir in one 6-ounce can frozen lemonade concentrate. Chill, stirring occasionally, till partially set.

Beat 3 egg whites till soft peaks form. Gradually add ½ cup sugar, beating to stiff peaks. Fold in gelatin mixture. Drain one 16-ounce can fruit cocktail. Reserving ½ cup fruit, fold remaining fruit into gelatin mixture. If necessary, chill till mixture mounds slightly when spooned. Pile into a *baked* 9-inch pastry shell, cooled (See *Pastry*). Chill till firm. Arrange reserved fruit in a ring atop pie. Trim with mint leaves, if desired.

Cranberry-Pear Pie

Prepare pastry for 9-inch lattice-top pie (See *Pastry*). Line 9-inch pie plate with pastry. Combine ½ cup sugar, 3 tablespoons all-purpose flour, ¼ teaspoon ground cinnamon, and dash salt. Blend with 1 tablespoon lemon juice and 1 cup whole cranberry sauce. Lightly stir in 3 cups sliced fresh pears. Turn into pastry-lined pie plate. Dot with 1 tablespoon butter.

Adjust lattice top. Seal; flute edge. Sprinkle top lightly with sugar. Cover pastry edge with foil. Remove foil a few minutes before pie is done. Bake at 400° for 35 to 40 minutes.

Cherry-Rhubarb Pie

A delectable blend of two fruits—

Prepare pastry for 9-inch lattice-top pie (See *Pastry*). In mixing bowl combine 1 pound rhubarb, cut in ½-inch slices (about 4 cups); one 16-ounce can pitted, tart red cherries (water pack), drained; 1¼ cups sugar; ¼ cup quick-cooking tapioca; and 5 drops red food coloring. Let stand 15 minutes. Line 9-inch pie plate with pastry; pour in filling. Adjust lattice top; seal and flute edge. Bake at 400° till done, 40 to 50 minutes. Serve pie while warm.

Accent the delectable flavor of Citrus-Cheese Pie with a garnish of fresh orange sections. Beneath the topping, lemon and orange team with cream cheese in this attractive dessert.

Uncooked pie fillings include some kinds of fluffy pies, some types of fruit pies such as strawberry pie, parfait pies, and ice cream, and other frozen pies. Convenience products, such as instant pudding mixes, can also be used for uncooked fillings. Most of these pies require chilling to make the pie filling hold its shape.

Vanilla-Raisin Pie

    1 cup raisins
  ½ teaspoon instant coffee powder
  ¼ teaspoon ground cinnamon
    Dash cloves
    1 3¾-ounce or 3⅝-ounce package
      instant vanilla pudding mix
1½ cups milk
    1 *baked* 8-inch pastry shell
      (See *Pastry*)
  ¼ cup chopped walnuts

Simmer raisins in ⅓ cup water in covered saucepan for 10 minutes. Stir in coffee powder, cinnamon, and cloves; cool. Beat pudding mix with milk for 30 seconds. Stir in raisin mixture. Pour into baked pastry shell. Sprinkle with chopped nuts. Chill thoroughly.

Date-Nut-Ice Cream Pie

    1 cup snipped pitted dates
  ½ cup sugar
  ½ cup chopped pecans
    1 tablespoon lemon juice
    Wafer Crust
    1 quart vanilla ice cream,
      softened

In saucepan combine dates, sugar, and ½ cup water. Heat to boiling; simmer 5 minutes. Add chopped pecans and lemon juice to hot date mixture; chill. Spread *half* the date mixture in Wafer Crust; cover with *half* the softened vanilla ice cream. Return to freezer to freeze ice cream. Repeat with remaining date filling and ice cream; freeze till firm. Remove from freezer 5 minutes before serving.

Wafer Crust: Combine 1½ cups fine vanilla wafer crumbs (36 wafers) and 6 tablespoons butter or margarine, melted. Press into a 9-inch pie plate; chill crust thoroughly.

Frozen Cranberry Velvet Pie

Especially refreshing as a summer dessert—

    Wafer Crust (see Date-Nut-
      Ice Cream Pie)
    1 8-ounce package cream cheese,
      softened
    1 cup whipping cream
  ¼ cup sugar
  ½ teaspoon vanilla
    1 16-ounce can whole cranberry
      sauce

       •   •   •

    Whipped cream

Prepare Wafer Crust; chill. Beat cream cheese till fluffy. Combine whipping cream, sugar, and vanilla; whip till thickened but not stiff. Gradually add to whipped cream cheese, beating till smooth and creamy. Set aside a few whole cranberries from sauce for garnish; fold remaining cranberry sauce into whipped mixture. Spoon filling into chilled crust; freeze till firm. Remove from freezer 10 minutes before serving. Top with additional whipped cream and the reserved berries. Makes 10 to 12 servings.

Pineapple Parfait Pie

An easy-to-make company dessert—

    Wafer Crust (see Date-Nut-
      Ice Cream Pie)
    1 8¾-ounce can crushed pineapple
    1 3-ounce package lemon-flavored
      gelatin
  ¼ cup cold water
    2 tablespoons lemon juice
    1 pint vanilla ice cream
    Whipped cream
    Pineapple slices

Prepare Wafer Crust; chill. Drain crushed pineapple, reserving syrup. Add enough water to syrup to make 1 cup; heat to boiling. Add gelatin to boiling liquid; stir till dissolved. Add cold water and lemon juice. Add ice cream by spoonfuls, stirring till melted. Chill till mixture mounds; fold in drained pineapple.

Pile pineapple filling into chilled crust. Chill till firm. Trim pie with whipped cream and pineapple slices.

Peanut–Ice Cream Pie

Prepare Graham Cracker Crust; reserve 1 to 2 tablespoons crumbs for garnish.

Whip ½ cup whipping cream. Soften 1 quart vanilla ice cream. Fold ½ cup crunchy peanut butter and whipped cream into ice cream. Quickly spoon mixture into crust. Sprinkle reserved graham cracker crumbs around edge. Freeze till firm, about 5 hours. Remove from freezer 10 to 15 minutes before serving.

Graham Cracker Crust: In mixing bowl combine 1¼ cups fine graham cracker crumbs, ¼ cup sugar, and 6 tablespoons melted butter or margarine. Press the crust firmly into 9-inch pie plate. Chill at least 45 minutes.

Irish Coffee Pie

In small mixer bowl combine one 3½-ounce package vanilla whipped dessert mix and 2 teaspoons instant coffee powder. Add ½ cup cold milk and beat at high speed of electric mixer for about 1 minute. Blend in ⅓ cup water and 3 tablespoons Irish whisky; beat at high speed till fluffy, about 2 minutes more. Whip ½ cup whipping cream; carefully fold into prepared filling. Pile into a *baked* 8-inch pastry shell, cooled (See *Pastry*). Chill 3 to 4 hours. Garnish with whipped cream and chocolate shavings.

Freezing pies

Fruit, general: Treat light-colored fruits with ascorbic acid color keeper. Prepare pie as usual but don't slit top crust. Cover unbaked pie with inverted paper plate. Wrap, seal, and freeze for up to 2 months. To bake, unwrap; cut vent holes in top crust. Bake, without thawing, at 450° to 475° for 15 to 20 minutes, then at 375° till done.

Apple, unbaked: Use firmer varieties of apples. Treat with ascorbic acid color keeper or steam slices 2 minutes, cool, and drain. Prepare and freeze as above. Store for up to 2 months. Unwrap; cut vent holes in top crust. Bake at 425° till done, about 1 hour.

Chiffon: Chocolate and lemon chiffon pies freeze satisfactorily. Freeze for up to 2 weeks. Thaw pie in refrigerator.

Family members and guests are sure to appreciate your choice of dessert when you serve them pie still warm from the oven. Of course, you don't always have enough time to make a pie while preparing dinner, so use a little forethought and keep several unbaked pies in the freezer. Making several pies at one time doesn't involve much more work than making one or two pies and, if you have pies in the freezer, you can fix dessert in the time it takes to put the pie in the oven.

Very often, one pie is more than enough for one meal, which necessitates storing the leftover pie until it is served again. Knowing where to store pies is no problem if you remember the following hints:

1. Refrigerate pies with fillings containing any eggs or dairy products.

2. Refrigerate pies that contain gelatin.

3. If necessary, fruit pies may be stored at room temperature for a short time.

With so many tasty pies to choose from, it is easy to serve pie often without serving the same kind. If your family is especially partial to one kind of fruit, try using that fruit in several different pies. For example, blueberries are equally delicious in two-crust fruit pies, fluffy chiffon pies, parfait pies, frozen pies, and cream pies. Remember also that savory fillings in a crust are as delicious as sweet fillings, so be sure to include meat and vegetable pies in your menus frequently.

PIE BIRD—A hollow, open-topped figurine designed to be inserted into the top crust of a two-crust pie to act as a steam vent. Originally shaped like a bird with an open beak, pie birds are made of ceramics.

PIECRUST—The pastry used in a pie. In recent years, piecrust mixes, to which you only need to add water, have become a popular shortcut for making pastry. Frozen piecrusts are also available. (See *Crust, Pastry* for additional information.)

PIE FILLING—The meat, vegetable, fruit, cream, custard, or other mixture put into a pie shell or between two piecrusts. Canned fruit and cream pie fillings need no further preparation before spooning into a crust or using in a recipe.

Ham with Cherry Sauce

    Large canned ham
1 10-ounce jar apple *or* guava jelly
1 tablespoon prepared mustard
⅓ cup pineapple juice
2 tablespoons dry white wine
1 21-ounce can cherry pie filling
½ cup light raisins

Heat the canned ham according to time on can. Half hour before end of heating time, remove ham and score fat in diamonds. In saucepan combine apple *or* guava jelly and mustard; stir in pineapple juice and dry white wine. Cook and stir to boiling; simmer 3 minutes. Pour ⅓ of glaze over ham; return to oven for 30 minutes. Spoon on glaze every 10 minutes.

    Heat pie filling and raisins to boiling; stir occasionally. Remove ham to platter. Add glaze from pan to cherry sauce. Bring to boil. Spoon some over ham. Pass remainder.

King Kamehameha Pie

1 12-ounce can pineapple juice
¾ cup sugar
7 medium cooking apples, peeled, cored, and cut in wedges (7 cups)
3 tablespoons cornstarch
1 tablespoon butter or margarine
½ teaspoon vanilla
1 *baked* 9-inch pastry shell (See *Pastry*)

In large saucepan combine 1¼ *cups* of the pineapple juice and the sugar. Bring to boiling. Add apple wedges. Simmer, covered, till tender but not soft, 3 to 4 minutes. Lift apples from syrup; set aside to drain. Combine cornstarch and remaining pineapple juice; add to syrup in saucepan. Cook and stir till thickened and bubbly; cook 1 minute more. Remove from heat; add butter, vanilla, and ¼ teaspoon salt. Cool 10 minutes without stirring.

    Pour about *half* the syrup into baked pastry shell, spreading to cover bottom. Arrange cooked apples atop. Spoon remaining syrup over apples. Cool thoroughly or chill. If desired, garnish pie with whipped cream or dairy sour cream and sprinkle with macadamia nuts.

Berry-Cheesecake Pie

1 8-ounce package cream cheese, softened
1 cup sifted confectioners' sugar
1 teaspoon vanilla
1 cup whipping cream
1 *baked* 9-inch pastry shell, cooled (See *Pastry*)
1 21-ounce can blueberry pie filling

Beat together first 3 ingredients till smooth. Whip cream; fold into cheese mixture. Spoon into pastry shell. Spoon pie filling atop. Chill.

Cherry-Chocolate Pie

1 4-ounce jar maraschino cherries
1 4-ounce package *regular* chocolate pudding mix
1 baked 9-inch pastry shell (See *Pastry*)
1 2-ounce package dessert topping mix
¼ cup chopped pecans

Drain cherries; reserve juice and chop cherries (should have about ¼ cup juice and ⅓ cup chopped cherries). Prepare pudding according to package directions using cherry juice and milk to make amount of liquid called for. Cool; pour into cooled pastry. Chill. Prepare topping according to package directions; fold in nuts and cherries. Spread atop pie.

PIE PAN—A round metal or glass baking container with sides that gently slope. Sizes are named according to diameter, which is measured from inside rim to inside rim. Popular pie pan sizes are eight and nine inches. Ten-inch pans are sometimes available, too. For well-filled pies, use the pie pan size specified in the recipe. Pie pans are also called pie tins.

PIEPLANT—An old-fashioned name for rhubarb. (See also *Rhubarb*.)

PIGEON—A small bird with a stout body and short legs. Young pigeons, sold as squabs, have tender meat. (See also *Squab*.)

PIGNOLIA—Another name for the pine nut. (See also *Pine Nut.*)

PIG'S EAR—The well-cleaned ear of a pig sometimes eaten fried, roasted, or cooked in a spicy tomato sauce.

PIG'S FEET—The portion of a pork leg below the knee and hock. Fresh, cured, and smoked pickled pig's feet are considered a delicacy by some people. These are often called pig's trotters.

PIGS IN A BLANKET—A frankfurter or sausage wrapped in pastry or dough and then baked. Miniature versions are made with cocktail franks and served as appetizers.

PIG'S KNUCKLE—The ankle joint or hock of a pork leg, which is commonly sold fresh, smoked, or pickled.

PIKE—A family of voracious freshwater fish. This fish commonly has a long body with a flattened back and small scales that cover the body. It has a large mouth with many sharp teeth and bottom jaws that protrude. All of the members of this family are sport fish and can put up quite a fight. The pike eats other game fish and often will eat small animals.

Some of the species of this family include common pike, muskellunge, and pickerel. Other species (varieties) of pickerel include western grass pickerel, redfin pickerel, and chain pickerel. Even though the walleye is sometimes called a pike or pikeperch, it actually belongs to the perch family.

The common pike lives in the lakes and rivers of North America and Europe. Other names for this fish include great northern pike and lake pike. It is a very quick fish when chasing its prey. A fully grown pike can measure up to four feet long. Whole pike that is sold weighs about three or four pounds. However, the pike that is found in markets is most often sold as fillets from the larger fish.

The muskellunge, often called muskie, is a larger species, often measuring five to eight feet long and weighing 100 pounds or more. The muskie likes medium-sized to large lakes and clear, cool, weedy waters.

The pickerel generally is smaller than the common pike. Pickerel is also the name of the young of the pike. The common market size ranges from 2 to 10 pounds. Pickerel is sold whole or as fillets.

Nutritional value: The three main species of the pike family, the northern pike, muskellunge, and pickerel, are all lean fish. A 3½-ounce portion of uncooked northern pike equals 88 calories, of pickerel equals 84 calories, and of muskellunge equals 109 calories. Like other fish, pike are good sources of high-quality protein.

How to store: Fresh pike should be kept refrigerated or iced and should be used within one or two days after it is caught or purchased. Frozen fish should not be stored any longer than six months.

How to prepare: Since all of the species of the pike family are lean fish, they are best if boiled, fried, or steamed. The flesh is firm, white, and flaky and has a good, sweet flavor. (See also *Fish.*)

PILAF, *(pi läf′, pē′ läf)*—Any of a variety of dishes in the cuisine of countries in India, Greece, Russia, and the Near, Middle, and Far East. Although numerous variations of pilaf exist, it is, basically, rice or cracked wheat cooked with seasonings and broth and served as an accompaniment to the main dish. A main dish pilaf is made by simply adding meat or poultry to the basic mixture.

The Greeks like butter and sometimes a touch of tomato paste in their simple rice pilaf. In India and the Far East, cinnamon, ginger, and curry powder are used as well as almonds to give an exotic flavor. In Syria and Lebanon the wheat pilaf may be served with a touch of yogurt, while the Turks often add a few cooked prunes and lemon slices to a lamb pilaf.

An easy company dish

Rolled chicken breasts top the flavorful rice → mixture in Chicken Pilaf. Convenience foods cut the preparation time to a minimum.

Chicken Pilaf

Subtly flavored with sherry—

        1 10½-ounce can condensed cream
            of mushroom soup
    1¼ cups boiling water
        ¼ cup dry sherry
        ½ envelope dry onion soup mix
            (¼ cup)
    1⅓ cups packaged precooked rice
        2 tablespoons chopped canned
            pimiento
        5 small chicken breasts
            Butter or margarine, melted
            Salt and pepper
            Paprika

In a 1½-quart casserole combine cream of mushroom soup, boiling water, dry sherry, onion soup mix, uncooked rice, and pimiento. Brush chicken breasts with butter; season with salt. pepper, and paprika. Place on top of rice. Cover; bake at 375° till chicken and rice are tender, about 1¼ hours. Makes 5 servings.

PILCHARD (*pil' cherd*)—A small, saltwater fish related to the herring. These fish have a slender, rounded body and oily flesh. They are native to the Mediterranean Sea, Atlantic coasts of Europe, the California coasts, and Japan.

The pilchard is used as a sardine. Excellent sardines imported from France and Portugal are pilchards. (See *Herring, Sardine* for additional information.)

PILOT BISCUIT—A large, hard, plain cracker served primarily with chowders and fish stews. They were formerly called hardtack or ship's biscuits because their good keeping quality made them suitable food for long ocean voyages.

PILSNER BEER (*pilz' nuhr, pils'*)—A light-bodied lager beer originally brewed in Pilsen, Czechoslovakia. (See also *Beer.*)

PIMENTO (*pi men' tō*)—The name given to allspice by early Spanish explorers, probably because the berry of the allspice tree somewhat resembles a large peppercorn. (See also *Allspice.*)

PIMIENTO (*pi myen' tō*)—A cone-shaped, sweet, red pepper with thick walls. Unlike this American definition identifying pimiento as a specific variety, the term *pimiento* in Spanish refers to a general group of mild-flavored peppers.

Pimiento peppers, processed in cans and jars, are available for home use in the United States. Commercially, they are also used in paprika seasoning.

Pimientos provide colorful decoration and subtle flavor to many recipes. They are a frequent garnish for vegetable salads and hot dishes, and for fish, cheese, or poultry casseroles. Pimiento pieces are a stunning addition to cream cheese, cottage cheese, and cheese dips and spreads. Some of the best-loved olives are stuffed with pimientos. (See also *Pepper.*)

Calico Vegetable Bowl

A colorful salad course—

        1 cup diced cooked potatoes
        1 cup diced cooked carrots
        1 cup cooked peas
        1 canned pimiento, chopped
        2 tablespoons chopped onion
        2 tablespoons snipped parsley
        ¼ cup French salad dressing
                    •   •   •
        ½ head lettuce
            Mayonnaise

Combine diced potatoes, diced carrots, peas, chopped pimiento, chopped onion, and parsley with French dressing. Chill 1 hour. Tear lettuce into bite-sized pieces; toss with other vegetables. Pass mayonnaise. Makes 6 servings.

Pimiento adds color and flavor to many dishes.

Tuna in Pepper Cups

      6 medium green peppers
    ¾ cup packaged precooked rice
      1 6½- or 7-ounce can tuna, drained
    ½ cup chopped celery
      2 tablespoons finely chopped onion
      2 tablespoons finely chopped canned
         pimiento
    ¾ cup mayonnaise or salad
         dressing
    ⅓ cup finely crushed potato chips

Cut peppers in half lengthwise; remove tops and seeds. Cook peppers in small amount boiling, salted water for 5 minutes; drain. Lightly sprinkle inside of peppers with salt.

Prepare rice according to package directions. Combine with tuna, celery, onion, and pimiento. Blend mayonnaise with ½ teaspoon salt and dash pepper; add to rice mixture and toss lightly. Spoon salad mixture into green pepper halves; sprinkle with finely crushed potato chips. Place peppers in 10x6x1¾-inch baking dish; pour about ⅓ cup water around peppers. Bake at 350° about 35 minutes Serves 6.

Beef and Noodles

      1 5½-ounce package noodles with
         sour cream-cheese sauce mix
      1 pound ground beef
    ½ cup chopped onion
      1 10½-ounce can condensed cream
         of mushroom soup
    ½ cup milk
      2 tablespoons chopped canned
         pimiento
    ¼ teaspoon dried thyme leaves,
         crushed
      1 cup soft bread crumbs
      2 tablespoons butter, melted
      2 ounces sharp Cheddar cheese,
         shredded (½ cup)

Prepare noodles with sauce mix according to package directions. Brown meat and onion in skillet. Stir in soup, milk, pimiento, thyme, and dash pepper. Add cooked noodles mixture. Turn into 10x6x1¾-inch baking dish. Combine crumbs and butter. Sprinkle atop casserole. Bake at 350° for 30 minutes. Sprinkle with cheese; bake 5 minutes longer. Serves 6.

Calico Chicken

      2 cups dairy sour cream
    ½ envelope dry onion soup mix
         (¼ cup)
      2 2½- to 3-pound ready-to-cook
         broiler-fryer chickens, cut up
      1 cup dry white wine
      1 teaspoon salt
    ½ teaspoon dried basil leaves,
         crushed
      2 cups uncooked long-grain rice
      1 10½-ounce can condensed cream
         of mushroom soup
    ¼ cup chopped canned pimiento
    ¼ cup snipped parsley

Combine sour cream and onion soup mix; chill. Place chickens in Dutch oven. Add 2 cups water, wine, salt, dash pepper, and basil. Cover; cook over low heat till tender, about 1 hour.

Meanwhile, cook rice following package directions. Remove chicken from broth; cool. Cut in large pieces. Cook liquid in Dutch oven, uncovered, till reduced to 1½ cups.

Blend in mushroom soup, pimiento, and parsley. Stir in sour cream mixture, chicken, and rice. Cook till heated. Serves 10 to 12.

Hamburger-Corn Bake

In large skillet cook 1½ pounds ground beef and 1 cup chopped onion till meat is lightly browned and onion is tender. Stir in one 12-ounce can whole kernel corn, drained; one 10½-ounce can condensed cream of chicken soup; one 10½-ounce can condensed cream of mushroom soup; 1 cup dairy sour cream; ¼ cup chopped canned pimiento; ¾ teaspoon salt; and ¼ teaspoon pepper. Mix well.

Stir in 6 ounces medium noodles (3 cups), cooked and drained. Turn into 2½-quart casserole. Mix 1 cup soft bread crumbs and 2 tablespoons melted butter; sprinkle atop. Bake at 350° about 45 minutes. Serves 8 to 10.

PIMM'S CUPS—Well-known, bottled English beverage mixtures that are served mixed with fruit juices in tall glasses. There are four Pimm's cups—No. 1 based on gin; No. 2 based on whisky; No. 3 based on rum; and No. 4 based on brandy.

PINEAPPLE—The cone-shaped fruit of a tropical plant botanically named *Ananus comosus*. The genus name *Ananus* is derived from a Paraguayan Indian word meaning excellent fruit. Spaniards named the fruit *pina de los Indies* (pinecone of the Indies) or *pina* for short, while the English coined the word pineapple.

A pineapple can be compared to an orchard because it is composed of many small fruits. After the plant's leaf cluster emerges from the ground, a stalk develops in the center of the leaf cluster. A cone with many eyes then emerges at the top of the stalk. Each eye of this cone produces a tiny blue and pink flower which, when pollinated, grows into a berry. As the berries ripen, they enlarge and merge together to form the familiar pineapple. At the same time that the berries are merging, another leaf cluster called the crown grows atop the cone-shaped fruit cluster.

Like many other fruits, pineapples have been enthusiastically received as food by many people. The wild plants, native to Brazil and Paraguay, were available to the ancient Guarani Indians of that region. As portions of the tribe moved to other parts of South America, they took pineapple plants with them and used the fruits for barter. By the time Columbus and his crew were introduced to pineapples, cultivation of pineapples was well established throughout Central and South America, and the Caribbean islands.

Although those pineapples taken back to Europe were well liked, it was not possible to grow the multifruited plants in the temperate European climate. Pineapples would not hold up well under shipping conditions, either. Consequently, they became rare delicacies. European horticulturists did attempt to grow pineapples in hothouses, but they were unsuccessful in their attempts until the early 1700s. By this time, however, ship handling techniques and storage facilities had improved greatly, thus, putting an end to the commercial venture in Europe.

Interestingly enough, pineapples also influenced the decor of seventeenth- and eighteenth-century Europe and America. In the tropics, pineapples were hung outside huts as tribal symbols of friendship and hospitality. In like manner, the pineapple motif was added to the tops of doorways, to gardens, furniture, china, and silver in Europe and the United States.

Today, Hawaii is the best-known and largest pineapple-producing region in the world, yet the first pineapples to reach those islands didn't arrive until the latter half of the eighteenth century. For many years thereafter, pineapple plants grew wild; some people even considered them weeds. The foundation for the growth of the pineapple industry came in 1886 when Captain John Kidwell, an English horticulturist, imported a commercial variety from Jamaica to Hawaii. The canning industry was subsequently developed in 1901 by James D. Dole.

How pineapples are produced: New pineapple plants are grown by inserting slips (from the fruit bases), suckers (from the lower stems) or crowns (from the tops of the fruits) of older plants into the soil. After the fields have been prepared, the soil is covered with plastic mulch. Holes are poked in the mulch, and the plants are inserted, allowing 15 to 18 thousand plants per acre. Pineapple planting was once a totally manual operation but, today, machines are used, too.

It takes about 15 months for a pineapple plant to flower and an additional three to seven months for the fruits to ripen. Pineapples are hand-harvested either mature but unripe (for fresh market) or fully ripe (for canning and freezing). After the first crop, pineapple plants are allowed to bear only two or three times more. Then, the plants are tilled under, and the planting cycle is repeated.

Nutritional value: Pineapples are best known nutritionally for their caloric and vitamin C content. Three-fourths cup of unsweetened, diced pineapple contains

Fruit-filled entrée

Iced pineapple halves, transformed into serv- →
ing dishes for Ham Salad-Fruit Boats, are coupled with an olive and parsley garnish.

Remove crown from fresh pineapple by holding crown in one hand and pineapple in the other. Twist each in reverse direction.

To prepare pineapple in the shell, quarter fruit and crown. Remove hard core. Cut fruit loose from the rind, then slice crosswise.

To remove rind, cut off base; stand upright. Slice from top to base in wide strips, cutting deep enough to remove most eyes.

only 52 calories. One serving (½ cup) provides a fair amount of vitamin C. Lesser amounts of other important vitamins and minerals are also present.

Types of pineapples: Although over 1500 plants belong to the pineapple family, many are far removed in appearance from the standard concept of a pineapple plant. The Spanish moss that grows profusely on trees in the southern United States, for example, is really a member of the pineapple family. Many other varieties are grown simply for their beauty.

Three main pineapple groups—Spanish, Cayenne, and Queen—are grown for their fruits. These groups differ greatly in appearance and flavor. Most of the varieties with these groups do not ship well and are utilized only in the localities where they are grown. Red Spanish, Smooth Cayenne, Queen, and Natal pineapples are most common to American markets.

In the Spanish group the best-known variety, the Red Spanish, is excellent for fresh shipment. The fruits are identified by crown leaves, which have sawtoothed edges. Rinds are yellow to reddish orange when ripe; the flesh is white.

The Smooth Cayenne in the Cayenne group is grown for both fresh and processed market. The large fruits are topped with smooth-edged leaves. The green and yellow rinds enclose soft, light yellow flesh.

The Queen and Natal pineapples in the Queen group are small fruit with reddish orange rinds. The flesh is deep yellow, almost pumpkin-colored, when ripe and is far sweeter than many other types.

How to select and store: The peak fresh pineapple crop is marketed from March through June, although in some parts of the country the fresh fruits are available year-round. Processed forms of pineapple are also available throughout the year.

When selecting fresh pineapples, look for the signs of ripeness and quality: plump, fresh looking, and good size; turning yellow or reddish brown; becoming slightly soft to the touch; developing a fruity, aromatic smell; and lacking decay signs at the base or sides. Avoid pineapples that have discolored or soft spots, as they are bruised. Other signs of decay are traces of mold, an unpleasant odor, and eyes that have turned dark in color and are watery. Pulling a leaf from the crown to see whether it comes out easily is a poor test for ripeness.

There is nothing to be gained by holding a pineapple at home in hopes it will improve in flavor and ripeness. The sooner it is eaten, the better. Uncut pineapple will keep in the refrigerator for a day or two; with rind and crown cut away, the flesh will keep a few days longer. How you refrigerate the fruit depends on whether or not the rind and crown will be used when serving the fruit.

There are many styles of processed pineapple to choose from: frozen pineapple chunks and juice; canned pineapple slices, chunks, tidbits, spears, juice and crushed pineapple. Syrup concentrations, from heavy syrup to juice- or water-pack, are available in many of these styles.

How to prepare: Pineapple preparation depends on how the fruit is to be served—in or out of the shell. If rind and crown are to be discarded, twist off crown and cut off base. Slice off strips of rind lengthwise, then remove eyes of fruit by cutting diagonal strips away. Cut away the hard core of the pineapple as you prepare spears, slices, chunks, or tidbits.

Pineapple served in the shell can be prepared as halves or quarters. For pineapple halves, cut in half lengthwise, crown and all. Remove any hard core. Cut around the edge of the fruit, leaving a rind about ½ inch thick. Cut loosened fruit crosswise, then lengthwise once or twice to make bite-sized pieces. Quarters are cut in the same way except the whole pineapple is cut into four lengthwise pieces.

How to use: Pineapple has become a multipurpose fruit because its flavor is agreeably inviting at all times of the day as well as in many different types of foods.

For breakfast, serve pineapple juice or cut fresh pineapple for openers. On special occasions, combine the juice with other fruit drinks, serve the fresh fruit atop your favorite cereal, or use fresh or processed pineapple in coffee cake.

Frosty Fruit Cup

With lime slush—

1 15-ounce can pineapple chunks (juice pack)
1 16-ounce bottle low-calorie lemon-lime carbonated beverage
2 tablespoons lime juice
   Few drops green food coloring

· · ·

1 cup seedless green grapes
2 cups cantaloupe balls
   Fresh mint sprigs

Drain pineapple chunks, reserving juice. Combine reserved pineapple juice, carbonated beverage, lime juice, and green food coloring; stir. Pour into a 3-cup refrigerator tray; freeze just to a mush, about 2 to 2½ hours. Combine pineapple, grapes, and cantaloupe. Break frozen mixture apart with fork, if necessary. Spoon into 8 sherbet glasses; top with fruits. Trim with mint sprigs. Makes 8 servings.

Pineapple provides refreshing taste in tossed or molded salads whether combined with other fruit, vegetables, or meats. Don't add fresh or frozen pineapple to gelatin without first cooking the pineapple. An enzyme present in fresh and frozen pineapple breaks down the gelatin and prevents it from setting.

Pineapple styles to know

Crushed: The pineapple is chopped into very small, irregular-sized pieces.

Chunks: Even, spoon-size-pieces cut from thick slices are available canned or frozen.

Tidbits: Slices are cut into small wedges that are more dainty than chunks.

Spears: Pineapple cylinders are cut in lengthwise strips.

Slices: Rings are cut crosswise from pineapple cylinders.

Allowing Pineapple Upside-Down Cake to cool about five minutes before inverting seals the fruit layer to the cake.

Upside-Down Pineapple Mold

   1 20-ounce can sliced pineapple
   1 3-ounce package lemon-flavored
     gelatin
   7 whole maraschino cherries
   2 cups finely chopped fresh
     rhubarb
  ½ cup water
  ⅓ cup sugar
   2 teaspoons lemon juice
   1 3-ounce package strawberry-
     flavored gelatin

Drain pineapple, reserving syrup. Add enough water to syrup to make 1½ cups; heat to boiling. Add to lemon gelatin and stir till dissolved. Chill till partially set; pour ½ *cup* in bottom of 6½-cup ring mold. Arrange pineapple slices over gelatin. Place a whole cherry in middle of each slice. Pour in remaining lemon gelatin. Chill till *almost* firm.

In saucepan combine rhubarb, water, and sugar. Cover and cook just till tender, about 5 minutes. Drain rhubarb thoroughly, reserving syrup. Add enough water to rhubarb syrup to make 1½ cups. Heat liquid to boiling. Stir in lemon juice and strawberry-flavored gelatin till dissolved. Chill till partially set; fold in reserved rhubarb. Pour over lemon layer in mold. Chill till firm. Unmold onto lettuce, if desired. Makes 10 to 12 servings.

Jellied Chicken Salad

Color and flavor packed—

   1 8¾-ounce can crushed pineapple
   2 envelopes unflavored gelatin
     (2 tablespoons)
  ½ cup cold water
   3 cups boiling chicken broth
  ¼ cup lemon juice
  ½ teaspoon salt
   2 cups diced cooked chicken
  ½ cup chopped celery
  ¼ cup chopped green pepper
   1 tablespoon chopped canned
     pimiento
    Mayonnaise or salad dressing

Drain pineapple, reserving syrup. Soften gelatin in cold water; dissolve in boiling chicken broth. Add reserved syrup, lemon juice, and salt. Chill till partially set.

Stir in drained pineapple, chicken, celery, green pepper, and pimiento. Pour into a 6½-cup ring mold; chill till firm. Serve with mayonnaise. Makes 8 to 12 servings.

Salmon-Fruit Mold

Try this unique combo—

   2 envelopes unflavored gelatin
     (2 tablespoons)
   2 tablespoons sugar
  ¼ cup lemon juice
   1 cup mayonnaise or salad
     dressing
   1 cup dairy sour cream
   1 7¾-ounce can salmon, drained,
     flaked, and bones removed
   1 8¾-ounce can crushed pineapple,
     undrained
   1 medium banana, thinly
     sliced (1 cup)
  ¾ cup chopped celery

In saucepan soften gelatin in 1 cup cold water; stir in sugar. Stir over low heat till gelatin and sugar are dissolved. Cool. Add lemon juice. Combine mayonnaise and sour cream; beat into cooled mixture till smooth. Fold in remaining ingredients. Pour into a 5½-cup mold; chill till firm. Makes 8 to 10 servings.

Beet-Pineapple Mold

    1 16-ounce can shoestring beets
    1 8¾-ounce can crushed pineapple
    2 3-ounce packages lemon-flavored
       gelatin
    2 cups boiling water
    2 tablespoons lemon juice
      Dash salt

Drain beets and pineapple, reserving 1½ cups of the combined liquids. Dissolve gelatin in boiling water; stir in reserved liquid, lemon juice, and salt. Chill till partially set, then fold in drained beets and pineapple. Pour gelatin mixture into a 6½-cup mold or eight to ten ½-cup molds. Chill till the gelatin mixture is firm. Makes 8 to 10 servings.

Ham Salad-Fruit Boats

    1 small pineapple, chilled
    1 cup cubed fully cooked ham
    ½ cup sliced celery
    1 tablespoon chopped green pepper
         •   •   •
    ¼ cup mayonnaise or salad dressing
    ½ teaspoon prepared mustard

Cut pineapple in half lengthwise. Remove hard core. Cut around edge of fruit, leaving a rim about ½ inch thick. Cut loosened fruit crosswise; remove and dice. Combine 1 cup of the diced pineapple with ham, celery, and green pepper. (Reserve remaining pineapple for another meal.) Blend mayonnaise and mustard; add to ham mixture. Toss to coat ingredients. Spoon into pineapple boats. Makes 2 servings.

Pineapple Dressing

Blend ⅓ cup sugar, 4 teaspoons cornstarch, and ¼ teaspoon salt; add 1 cup pineapple juice, ¼ cup orange juice, and 3 tablespoons lemon juice. Cook and stir till thickened and bubbly. Cook 2 minutes more. Add small amount of hot mixture to 2 beaten eggs. Return to hot mixture. Cook and stir over low heat till slightly thickened, about 3 to 5 minutes.

    Cool thickened mixture for 5 minutes. Beat into two 3-ounce packages cream cheese, softened. Chill. Makes 2⅓ cups dressing.

Polynesian and oriental cooks have devised many vegetable dishes and main dishes utilizing pineapple. Sweet-sour dishes are the most well known of these.

Polynesian Yam Casserole

    1 18-ounce can yams, drained
       and sliced
    1 medium banana, thickly sliced
    1 8¾-ounce can pineapple tidbits
    ¼ teaspoon salt
    ¼ cup flaked coconut

Arrange yams and banana in a 10x6x1¾-inch baking dish. Pour pineapple with syrup over all (be sure banana is moistened). Sprinkle with salt. Bake, uncovered, at 350° for 15 minutes. Sprinkle with coconut; continue baking 15 minutes longer. Makes 4 servings.

Turkey Hawaiian

A meal-in-one dish—

    ½ cup chopped onion
    2 tablespoons butter or margarine
    1 10-ounce package frozen peas
  1½ cups diagonally sliced celery
    1 3-ounce can broiled sliced
       mushrooms
    2 chicken bouillon cubes
         •   •   •
    1 tablespoon cornstarch
    1 tablespoon soy sauce
         •   •   •
    1 13½-ounce can pineapple tidbits,
       drained
    1 5-ounce can water chestnuts,
       drained and sliced
    2 cups diced cooked turkey
      Hot cooked rice
    ½ cup toasted slivered almonds

Cook onion in butter till tender. Stir in peas, celery, mushrooms, bouillon cubes, and 1 cup water; bring to boil. Cover; simmer 5 minutes. Combine cornstarch and soy sauce; stir into mixture. Cook and stir till mixture boils. Add pineapple, water chestnuts, and turkey; heat through. Serve on hot rice; top with almonds. Pass additional soy sauce. Serves 5 or 6.

Sweet and Sour Franks

 1 8¾-ounce can pineapple
   tidbits
 2 tablespoons butter or margarine
 ½ cup chopped onion
 1 medium green pepper, cut in
   1-inch strips

 •   •   •

 1 beef bouillon cube
 1 cup boiling water
 2 tablespoons cornstarch
 1 tablespoon brown sugar
   Dash salt
 2 tablespoons vinegar
 1 tablespoon soy sauce
 ½ pound frankfurters, sliced
   crosswise
   Hot cooked rice

Drain pineapple, reserving syrup. In skillet melt butter. Add onion and green pepper; cover and cook over low heat for 5 minutes.

Dissolve bouillon cube in boiling water. Mix cornstarch, brown sugar, and salt; add pineapple syrup, vinegar, soy, and bouillon. Pour over vegetables. Cook and stir till thickened and bubbly. Add frankfurters and pineapple. Heat. Serve over rice. Makes 4 servings.

Miniature Pineapple Puffs are made from convenience foods—piecrust mix, whipped dessert topping, and pineapple preserves.

Pineapple desserts can be plain or fancy. Serve the fresh fruit in pineapple boats bedded in crushed ice or in elegant fruit combinations. When interest seems to be waning, add pineapple upside-down cake, pineapple cookies, pies, or sherbet to the menu. (See also *Fruit*.)

Frosty Pineapple Dessert

Partially thaw one 13½-ounce can frozen pineapple chunks and break apart. Put the pineapple chunks in blender container. Cover; blend at low speed, stopping blender to scrape down sides occasionally. Blend 2 minutes or till the dessert is slushy. Makes 3 servings.

Pineapple-Lime Float

 1 12-ounce can unsweetened pineapple juice (1½ cups)
 1 cup lime juice
 ⅔ cup sugar
   Few drops green food coloring
 1 pint lime sherbet
 2 7-ounce bottles ginger ale,
   chilled (about 2 cups)

Combine pineapple juice, lime juice, sugar, and green food coloring; chill. Fill 6 glasses half full with lime mixture; add a scoop of sherbet to each. Fill with ginger ale. Garnish with fresh mint if desired. Makes 6 servings.

Peach and Pineapple Shake

 1 cup sliced fresh peaches*
 ¼ cup unsweetened pineapple juice,
   chilled
 ¼ cup sugar
 1 pint vanilla *or* peach ice cream
 ¾ cup milk

Place peaches, pineapple juice, and sugar in blender container. Cover; blend at high speed till smooth (about 10 seconds). Add ice cream; blend till the ice cream is softened. Add milk, mixing just till blended. Pour into 2 chilled tall glasses. Makes 2 servings.

*Or use ¾ cup drained, canned sliced peaches and omit sugar in recipe.

Fresh Pineapple Jubilee

A flaming spectacle—

    ½ cup orange marmalade
    2 tablespoons light corn syrup
    2 tablespoons brown sugar
    2 cups diced fresh pineapple
        •   •   •
    ¼ cup orange-flavored liqueur
      Vanilla ice cream

Combine orange marmalade, corn syrup, and brown sugar in blazer pan of chafing dish; stir in diced pineapple. Heat over direct heat till warm. Heat orange liqueur in ladle or small pan; ignite and pour over pineapple mixture. Spoon sauce over scoops of ice cream in individual sherbets. Makes 2 cups sauce.

Pineapple Upside-Down Cake

Bake this delicious cake in either a round or square pan—

    1 8½-ounce can sliced pineapple
    3 tablespoons butter
    ½ cup brown sugar
    4 maraschino cherries, halved
        •   •   •
    ⅓ cup shortening
    ½ cup granulated sugar
    1 egg
    1 teaspoon vanilla
        •   •   •
    1 cup sifted all-purpose flour
    1¼ teaspoons baking powder
    ¼ teaspoon salt

Drain pineapple, reserving syrup. Halve pineapple slices. Melt butter in 9x1½-inch round *or* 8x8x2-inch pan. Add brown sugar and 1 *tablespoon* of the reserved pineapple syrup. Add water to remaining syrup to make ½ cup. Arrange pineapple in the bottom of pan. Place a cherry half in center of each slice.

Cream together shortening and sugar till light. Add egg and vanilla; beat till fluffy. Sift together dry ingredients; add alternately with the ½ *cup* reserved pineapple syrup, beating after each addition. Spread over pineapple. Bake at 350° for 40 to 45 minutes. Cool 5 minutes; invert on plate. Serve while warm.

Tiny Pineapple Upside-Down Cakes

    1 8¾-ounce can pineapple tidbits
    3 tablespoons butter or margarine
    ½ cup brown sugar
    4 maraschino cherries, halved
    1 1-layer-size yellow cake mix

Drain pineapple, reserving syrup. Melt butter or margarine; stir in *1 tablespoon* of the reserved syrup. Place ½ *tablespoon* of the butter mixture into each of eight 6-ounce custard cups. Add *1 tablespoon* of the brown sugar to each. Arrange pineapple tidbits in custard cups atop brown sugar, using 3 or 4 tidbits for each. Center each cup with a cherry half.

Prepare cake mix according to package directions, using remaining reserved pineapple syrup, plus enough water to equal liquid called for on package. Divide batter among the custard cups, using about ¼ cup for each. Bake at 350° for 30 to 35 minutes. Let stand 5 minutes before inverting onto serving plate. Serve warm. Makes 8 servings.

Pineapple Chiffon Cake

    2¼ cups sifted cake flour
    1½ cups sugar
    3 teaspoons baking powder
    ½ cup salad oil
    5 egg yolks
    ¾ cup unsweetened pineapple juice
    1 cup egg whites (8)
    ½ teaspoon cream of tartar
      Pineapple-Whipped Topping

Sift together flour, sugar, baking powder, and 1 teaspoon salt into bowl. Make well in center and add *in order*: salad oil, egg yolks, and pineapple juice. Beat until satin smooth.

In large mixing bowl beat egg whites with cream of tartar till *very stiff peaks* form. Pour batter in thin stream over entire surface of egg whites; fold in gently. Bake in *ungreased* 10-inch tube pan at 350° about 1 hour. Invert; cool. Split cooled cake into 2 layers. Fill with part of Pineapple-Whipped Topping; frost top and sides with remainder.

Pineapple-Whipped Topping: Thoroughly drain one 20½-ounce can crushed pineapple, chilled. Whip 2 cups whipping cream. Fold drained pineapple into whipped cream.

Pineapple-Sour Cream Pie

    ¾ cup sugar
    ¼ cup all-purpose flour
    ½ teaspoon salt
    1 20½-ounce can crushed pine-
       apple, undrained
    1 cup dairy sour cream
    1 tablespoon lemon juice
    2 slightly beaten egg yolks
            · · ·
    1 *baked* 9-inch pastry shell
       (See *Pastry*)
       Meringue

In saucepan combine sugar, flour, and salt. Stir in pineapple, sour cream, and lemon juice. Cook and stir till mixture thickens and comes to a boil; cook 2 minutes. Stir small amount of hot mixture into egg yolks; return to hot mixture, stirring constantly. Cook and stir 2 minutes. Spoon into cooled pastry shell. Spread Meringue atop pie, sealing meringue to crust, and bake at 350° for 12 to 15 minutes.

Meringue: Beat 2 egg whites with ½ teaspoon vanilla and ¼ teaspoon cream of tartar till soft peaks form. Gradually add ¼ cup sugar, beating till stiff peaks form and sugar dissolves.

Shape lengthwise bread slices into Polka-Dot Pinwheels by rolling jelly-roll fashion. Slice the tea sandwiches ⅜ inch thick.

Fresh Pineapple Pie

       Plain Pastry for 2-crust 9-inch
          pie (See *Pastry*)
    ¾ cup sugar
    3 tablespoons quick-cooking
       tapioca
    4 cups fresh pineapple chunks
    1 teaspoon grated lemon peel
    1 tablespoon lemon juice
    1 tablespoon butter or margarine

Line 9-inch pie plate with half of pastry. Mix sugar, tapioca, and dash salt; add pineapple, lemon peel, and juice. Let stand 15 minutes. Turn into pastry-lined plate. Dot with butter. Adjust top crust, cutting slits for escape of steam; seal. Bake at 425° about 45 minutes.

Pineapple Puffs

    1 stick piecrust mix
    2 eggs
    1 tablespoon chopped candied
       ginger
    1 cup frozen whipped dessert
       topping, thawed
       Pineapple preserves

Add piecrust mix to ⅔ cup boiling water; stir till pastry forms a ball. Cook and stir 1 minute. Place in mixer bowl; add eggs. Beat 2 minutes on low speed. Drop from a teaspoon onto greased and floured baking sheet. Bake at 400° for 15 to 20 minutes. Split puffs; cool.

Fold candied ginger into dessert topping. Mound topping on split puffs. Top each puff half with a dab of preserves. Makes about 50.

PINEAPPLE CHEESE—A full-flavored Cheddar cheese that is molded and marked to resemble a miniature pineapple. The deep yellow wax coating increases its appearance similarity to the fruit. This American-made cheese was first produced in Litchfield County, Connecticut, around 1845. (See also *Cheddar Cheese*.)

PINE NUT—A seed from the cone of one of several pine tree varieties that grow in the southwestern United States, Mexico, and southern Europe. Thin, light brown shells cover the soft, creamy white interiors of these cylindrical nuts that average ¼ inch in length.

Called *piñon* by Indians and *pignolia* by Italians, mild-flavored pine nuts are suitable to use with many different foods. Roasted and sometimes salted, they can serve as a garnish for salads and vegetables, as an ingredient in cakes, pastries, and candies, or can be eaten plain as a snack. They frequently appear in Mediterranean dishes. (See also *Nut*.)

PINTO BEAN—A brown-speckled beige bean. Pinto beans are grown mainly in western states and used extensively in the southwestern United States. (See also *Bean*.)

Texas-Style Beans

> 2 cups pinto beans
> 1 cup chopped onion
> ¼ pound salt pork, diced
> 1 clove garlic, minced
> 2 teaspoons salt
> 2 16-ounce cans tomatoes
> ¾ cup diced green pepper
> 6 drops bottled hot pepper sauce
> 1 tablespoon sugar
>   Perfect Corn Bread

Cover beans with water; soak the beans overnight. *Do not drain* them. Add onion, salt pork, garlic, salt, and a dash pepper. Cook, covered, over low heat for 2 hours. Add tomatoes, green pepper, hot pepper sauce, and sugar. Cook the mixture, covered, for 3 hours

Serve over *Perfect Corn Bread:* Sift together 1 cup sifted all-purpose flour, ¼ cup sugar, 4 teaspoons baking powder, and ¾ teaspoon salt. Stir in 1 cup yellow cornmeal. Add 1 cup milk, 2 eggs, and ¼ cup softened shortening. Beat with rotary or electric beater just till smooth, 1 minute. (Do not overbeat.) Pour into greased 9x9x2-inch baking pan. Bake at 425° for 20 to 25 minutes. Serves 8 to 10.

PINWHEEL—A cookie or sandwich made by rolling up dough or bread that is spread with a filling. When sliced, the cookie or sandwich has the concentric-circle appearance of a spinning pinwheel.

Polka-Dot Pinwheels

Teatime goodies—

Have bakery cut 1 loaf unsliced white bread into lengthwise slices about ¼ inch thick. Spread 4 slices of the bread with softened butter or margarine. Combine one 4¾-ounce can chicken spread, 2 tablespoons mashed canned pimiento, and ¼ teaspoon curry powder.

Spread *each* slice buttered bread with about 3 tablespoons filling. Trim crusts. Place 5 *thin* green pepper strips, equal distance apart, on filling on each slice. Roll up, beginning at narrow end. Wrap rolls in foil or clear plastic wrap; chill. Slice into ⅜-inch pinwheels. Makes about 20 pinwheels. (To use whole loaf bread, double amount of filling.)

PIP—The seed of a fruit such as an apple, orange, or lemon.

PIPE—To decorate food by extruding another semisolid food through a decorative pastry tube. Frosting is often piped onto cakes for special occasions. Fluffy duchess potatoes are quite often piped around the steak for planked steak.

PIPERADE *(pē pä räd')*—An omeletlike dish that originated in the Basque area of southwestern France consisting of eggs, green pepper, tomato, and onion.

PIQUANT *(pē' kuhnt, -känt)*—The taste quality of a food that is pleasingly sharp, stimulating to the taste buds, and satisfying to the palate.

PIQUANTE SAUCE—A brown sauce variation with shallots, wine or vinegar, capers, and pickles as added ingredients. This sauce makes an excellent topping for sliced pork, beef, and leftover meats. (See also *Brown Sauce*.)

PIROSHKI *(pi rôsh' kē)* **PIROGEN** *(pi rō' guhn)*—Small, fingerlike, filled pastries common to Russian cuisine. These piecrust-, yeast-, or puff paste-based pastries may contain any number of fillings featuring meat, fish, cheese, rice, egg, and mushrooms. (See also *Russian Cookery*.)

PISANG GORENG—The Indonesian name for fried bananas. These are delicious served as a meat accompaniment.

Pisang Goreng

> 8 large, all-yellow bananas
> 2 tablespoons lemon juice
> ½ cup brown sugar
> ½ cup salad oil

Peel bananas and halve lengthwise. (If bananas are extra large, cut again in halves crosswise.) Brush with lemon juice and roll in brown sugar. Heat salad oil in skillet; add bananas and fry till golden brown, about 2 minutes. Serve very hot. Makes 8 servings.

PISCO (*pis'-kō, pē' skō*)—A potent, Peruvian brandy that is made from grapes.

PISSALADIÈRE (*pē sä lä dyâr'*)—A French word for a tart that is made of a brioche dough crust filled with a flavorful mixture of anchovies, onions, ripe olives, and other vegetables. This pizzalike dish is a specialty of Nice, France.

PISTACHIO NUT (*pi sta͟sh' ē ō, -stä' s͟hē ō'*)—The seed of the fruit of a small evergreen tree related to the sumac. These almond-flavored nuts are grown primarily in the Near Eastern and Mediterranean regions. In this country, there is a small crop of pistachio nuts grown in California.

Two colors—red and green—are characteristically associated with pistachio nuts. The thin, oval shell of pistachio nuts is naturally beige, but when the nuts are salted and sun-roasted, the shell turns reddish pink. Today, sun-roasting has been largely replaced by mechanical roasting, which doesn't change the color of the shell. Often, however, the shell is dyed to imitate the expected color. The distinctive, light green color of the edible kernel makes pistachio nuts useful as a coloring as well as a flavoring agent.

Roasted and salted pistachio nuts are particularly enjoyed right from the shell and in dishes such as candies, baked goods, and ice cream. (See also *Nut*.)

Cheese-Nut Mold

> 1 3-ounce package lime-flavored gelatin
> 1 7-ounce bottle ginger ale, chilled (about 1 cup)
> 1 12-ounce carton small curd cream-style cottage cheese, well drained
> 1 tablespoon mayonnaise or salad dressing
> ¼ cup chopped pistachio nuts

Dissolve gelatin in 1 cup boiling water. Cool; gently stir in ginger ale. Chill till partially set. Combine cottage cheese, mayonnaise or salad dressing, and pistachio nuts; fold into gelatin. Pour into a 3½-cup mold. Chill till firm. Makes 4 to 6 servings.

PIT—1. The seed of a fruit such as a peach or apricot. 2. To remove this seed.

PIZZA—The Italian word for pie, now specifically applied to a spicy, open-faced pie traditionally topped with tomatoes, cheese, and herbs. The flavorful topping usually contains other ingredients such as onion, green pepper, mushrooms, sausage, ground beef, or anchovies.

This hearty food originated in Naples, Italy, where it was a specialty as long ago as the sixteenth century. At that time, King Ferdinand enjoyed pizza so much that he persuaded a renowned pizza chef to bake pizzas especially for him and his court. In fact, the king was so enthusiastic about this main dish that he insisted on licking his fingers rather than using a napkin.

Although the popularity of pizza spread rapidly throughout Italy, most Americans were not familiar with this dish until after World War II when soldiers returning home from Italy brought recipes and a taste for pizza with them. Today, this tasty pie with its countless variations is an all-American favorite.

An integral part of the American pizza is a thin, crispy crust, unlike the thick crust of Italian pizzas. Most pizza crusts contain yeast and are made like other yeast breads. Often, however, many of the time-consuming tasks associated with making yeast breads are eliminated by using packaged pizza mixes or convenience ingredients such as hot roll or biscuit mixes.

One of the attractions of many restaurants specializing in pizzas is watching the chef shape the dough by alternately shaping it with his hands and flipping it into the air. Although this method is spectacular, it takes a lot of practice to perfect. Therefore, most homemakers are better off rolling or patting the dough.

Preparing a topping for pizza is one area in which the creative cook excels. Starting with ingredients like tomatoes (fresh, canned, sauce, or paste), onions, green peppers, ripe and pimiento-stuffed olives, mushrooms, shrimp, Canadian bacon, sausage, ground beef, ham, anchovies, cheese, or anything else that sounds good, you can come up with numerous combinations that will delight any guest.

Even the cheese you use can add variety to your pizzas. Favorite pizza cheeses include mozzarella, Parmesan, and romano, but almost any cooking cheese is suitable. Since the "stringiness" of natural cheese is expected on pizza, make sure that you use a natural rather than a process cheese. (See also *Italian Cookery*.)

Homemade Pizza Crust

      1   package active dry yeast
      1   cup *warm* water (110°)
· · ·
   3½   cups sifted all-purpose flour
      3   tablespoons salad oil
      1   teaspoon salt

Soften yeast in water. Beat in *1½ cups* flour; mix in *1 tablespoon* salad oil and salt. Stir in remaining flour. Knead till smooth and elastic, about 12 minutes (will be firm). Place in lightly greased bowl; turn greased side up. Cover. Let rise till more than double, 1½ to 2 hours. Punch down and cover; chill.

Cut dough in half. On lightly floured surface, roll each half into a 12-inch circle, about ⅛ inch thick. Place in two greased 12-inch pizza pans, forming edges. With knuckles, dent dough. Brush dough circles with remaining salad oil. Fill. Bake at 425° for 20 to 25 minutes. Makes two 12-inch pizza crusts.

Biscuit Pizza Crust

      1   package active dry yeast
      ¾   cup *warm* water (110°)
· · ·
   2½   cups packaged biscuit mix
            Olive oil *or* salad oil

Soften yeast in warm water (110°). Add biscuit mix; beat vigorously for 2 minutes. Dust surface with biscuit mix; knead dough till smooth (25 strokes). Divide dough in half and roll each piece to a 12-inch circle.

Place dough circles on greased baking sheets; crimp edges of the dough. Brush dough with oil. Fill. Bake at 425° till done, about 15 minutes. Makes two 12-inch pizza crusts.

Jiffy Pizza Crust

      1   13¾-ounce package hot roll
            mix
            Salad oil

Using *1 cup warm water* (110°) and *no egg*, prepare hot roll mix according to package directions. *Do not let rise.* Cut in half.

With oiled hands, pat each half of dough into 12-inch circle on greased baking sheet. Clip edge at 1-inch intervals; press so edge stands up. Brush with salad oil. Fill. Bake at 450° till done, about 15 to 20 minutes. Makes two 12-inch pizza crusts.

Using the palm of your hand and your fingers, press the pizza dough onto a greased baking sheet or a circular pizza pan.

Sausage Pizza

A teen-age favorite—

> **Pizza Crust**
> . . .
> 1 pound Italian sausage
> 1 16-ounce can tomatoes
> Salt
> Pepper
> 1 6-ounce package mozzarella
>   cheese, thinly sliced and torn
>   in pieces
> 2 tablespoons olive oil
> . . .
> 1 6-ounce can tomato paste
> 2 cloves garlic, minced
> 1 tablespoon dried oregano leaves,
>   crushed
> 1 tablespoon whole basil
> Salt
> Pepper
> ¼ cup grated Parmesan *or* romano
>   cheese
> 2 tablespoons olive oil

Using recipe for Biscuit Pizza Crust, Home-made Pizza Crust, *or* Jiffy Pizza Crust, prepare two 12-inch pizza-dough circles. Set aside.

In skillet break Italian sausage in bits. Cook slowly till lightly browned, about 10 minutes, stirring occasionally; drain off fat. Drain tomatoes, reserving ½ cup juice. Cut tomatoes in small pieces and layer on prepared pizza-dough circles. Sprinkle with salt and pepper; then cover with mozzarella cheese. Using 2 tablespoons olive oil, drizzle oil over both pizzas. Sprinkle with browned sausage.

In mixing bowl combine tomato paste, reserved tomato juice, minced garlic, crushed oregano, and whole basil. Mix thoroughly; spread over sausage. Dash generously with salt and pepper. Scatter grated Parmesan *or* romano cheese atop. Drizzle pizzas with remaining 2 tablespoons olive oil. Bake at 425° till crusts are done, about 15 minutes. Makes 2 pizzas.

Pizza galore

← From top: Pepperoni Pizza, packaged pizza with anchovies and cheese, Sausage Pizza, and Cheese Pizza suit a variety of tastes.

Sausage-Salami Pizza

> ½ pound Italian *or* bulk pork
>   sausage
> 1 clove garlic, crushed
> 1 teaspoon *each* dried oregano and
>   dried basil leaves, crushed
> 1 package cheese pizza mix
>   (for 1 pizza)
> 1 3-ounce can sliced mushrooms,
>   drained (½ cup)
> 1 6-ounce package mozzarella
>   cheese, cut in thin pieces
> 6 salami slices

In skillet break sausage in small bits. Brown slowly. Drain. Add garlic, oregano, and basil.

Prepare pizza crust according to directions. Roll or pat out to fit 12-inch pizza pan. Crimp edges. Shake on *half* the grated cheese from mix package; cover with pizza sauce (from mix package), sausage mixture, remaining grated cheese, mushrooms, then mozzarella cheese. Bake at 425° 15 to 20 minutes.

Roll salami slices in cone shape. Arrange in center of pizza. If desired, garnish with pimiento-stuffed green olives and sprigs of parsley. Makes one 12-inch pizza.

Ground Beef Pizza

> 1½ pounds ground beef
> 1 small clove garlic, minced
> 1 teaspoon dried oregano leaves,
>   crushed
> 2 8-ounce cans tomato sauce with
>   mushrooms
> 2 12-inch pizza-dough circles
> 1 small onion, sliced and
>   separated into rings
> 1 medium green pepper, cut
>   into rings
> 1 6-ounce package sliced mozzarella
>   cheese, torn in pieces
> ¼ cup grated Parmesan cheese

In skillet brown beef; drain off excess fat. Add garlic and oregano. Spread tomato sauce over pizza-dough circles; top with meat. Arrange onion and green pepper rings atop meat. Cover with mozzarella cheese, then sprinkle with Parmesan. Bake according to directions for crust. Makes two 12-inch pizzas.

Short-Cut Pizza

A great use for leftover meat loaf—

- 1 package cheese pizza mix (for 1 pizza)
- ½ teaspoon dried oregano leaves, crushed
- ¼ teaspoon garlic powder
- 2 cups crumbled leftover meat loaf
- 1 3-ounce can sliced mushrooms, drained (½ cup)
- 1 4-ounce package shredded pizza cheese (1 cup)

Prepare pizza dough following package directions. Roll or pat out to fit 12-inch pizza pan. Place in greased 12-inch pizza pan; crimp edges. Blend oregano and garlic powder with pizza sauce (from package mix); spread over pizza dough. Cover with crumbled meat loaf, mushrooms, then pizza cheese. Sprinkle the grated cheese (from package mix) atop. Bake at 425° till crust is done, about 20 minutes. Makes one 12-inch pizza.

Mushroom-Cheese Pizza

Even the crust is cheesy—

In saucepan cook ¼ cup finely chopped onion and 1 clove garlic, minced, in 2 tablespoons salad oil till tender. Stir in one 6-ounce can sliced mushrooms, undrained; *half* of a 6-ounce can tomato paste (⅓ cup); 1 teaspoon brown sugar; ½ teaspoon dried basil leaves, crushed; ¼ teaspoon salt; and ⅛ teaspoon pepper. Heat, stirring the mixture occasionally.

In mixing bowl combine 1¼ cups packaged biscuit mix, ¼ cup grated Parmesan cheese, and ¼ teaspoon dried oregano leaves, crushed. Add ⅓ to ½ cup milk to make a soft dough. Turn dough out onto a cloth dusted with biscuit mix; knead 8 to 10 strokes. Press dough into a 12-inch circle on a greased pizza pan or baking sheet, forming rim around edge. Spread the mushroom mixture over the dough to rim. Sprinkle with ¼ cup grated Parmesan cheese. Bake at 400° till crust is brown, about 18 to 20 minutes. Top the pizza with 3 ounces mozzarella cheese, cut in very thin strips, during last few minutes of baking.

Cheese Pizza

A delicious no-meat pizza—

- 1 package active dry yeast
- ¾ cup *warm* water (110°)
- 2½ cups packaged biscuit mix
  Olive oil

. . .

- 1 pound mozzarella cheese, thinly sliced
- 1 chopped onion
- ½ cup chopped green pepper
- 1 6-ounce can broiled sliced mushrooms, drained
  Salt

. . .

- 3 5½-ounce cans pizza sauce (2¼ cups)
  Coarsely ground pepper
  Dried oregano leaves, crushed
  Yellow and red pickled banana peppers

In mixing bowl soften yeast in warm water (110°). Add packaged biscuit mix; beat vigorously 2 minutes. On surface dusted with biscuit mix, knead till smooth, about 25 strokes. Divide dough in fourths. On greased baking sheets, roll each fourth paper-thin to a 10-inch circle or pat into four 9-inch pizza pans; turn up edges of dough and crimp, if desired. Brush dough with olive oil.

Cut part of the mozzarella cheese into 16 thin triangles; set aside for trim. Tear remaining mozzarella cheese in pieces and scatter over prepared pizza crusts.

Sprinkle chopped onion, chopped green pepper, and broiled sliced mushrooms over cheese layer; dash with salt. Drizzle pizza sauce over; dash generously with coarsely ground pepper and crushed oregano. Arrange reserved cheese triangles atop pizzas. Cut yellow and red banana peppers into triangles and arrange atop the cheese. Bake at 425° till crust is done, about 15 minutes. Makes 4 pizzas.

Pizza fix-up

A convenient packaged cheese pizza mix becomes an extra-special dish when you make it into this hearty Sausage-Salami Pizza.

Pepperoni Pizza

    2 8-ounce cans tomato sauce
    ½ cup chopped onion
    2 to 3 teaspoons dried oregano
        leaves, crushed
    1 teaspoon aniseed
    2 cloves garlic, minced
    2 12-inch pizza-dough circles
    8 ounces pepperoni, thinly sliced
    2 6-ounce packages mozzarella
        cheese, cut in thin pieces

Mix first 5 ingredients, ½ teaspoon salt, and dash pepper; spread over the two 12-inch pizza-dough circles. Scatter pepperoni slices over the crusts, reserving some pepperoni for trim. Add cheese. Top the pizza with reserved pepperoni. Bake according to directions for crust. Makes two 12-inch pizzas.

PLAICE *(plās)*—A lean, saltwater flatfish belonging to the flounder family. The plaice is distinguished from other fish in the flounder family by the red and orange spots found on its gray brown skin. This flavorful fish lives in both European waters and off the United States' east coast. The plaice averages between 12 and 18 inches long. (See also *Flounder.*)

PLANKED STEAK—Broiled steak and vegetable accompaniments served on a wooden plank. Originally an idea of the American Indian, the plank may also be used for fish.

Since the plank is an integral part of this cooking technique, choose and prepare it carefully. Select a hardwood plank, preferably oak, maple, or hickory. Before using the plank, brush it well with salad oil and heat it in a 300° oven for 1 hour.

A thick, juicy steak surrounded by a border of Duchess potatoes, peas, French-fried onions, broiled tomatoes, and carrots makes up Planked Steak. Serving style accounts for name.

Planked Steak

> Porterhouse, T-bone, or sirloin
>   steak, cut 1½ inches thick
> Duchess Potatoes
> Butter
> Hot buttered vegetables
> Parsley

Slash fatty edge of steak. Place on broiler rack; broil top side 3 inches from heat (7 to 8 minutes for rare, 9 to 10 minutes for medium, and 12 to 15 minutes for well-done). Season with salt and pepper. Turn; broil other side (2 minutes for rare, 3 minutes for medium, and 5 to 8 minutes for well-done). Place steak on seasoned plank.

Pipe border of Duchess Potatoes around edge of plank. (To match picture, form loops to hold vegetables.) Melt 2 tablespoons butter and drizzle over potatoes. Oil exposed wood. Broil 4 inches from heat till potatoes brown and meat is done, about 5 to 7 minutes.

Remove from broiler; add hot buttered vegetables and parsley. Top steak with a pat or two of butter. Place plank on serving tray.

Duchess Potatoes: Beat 1 tablespoon butter, 1 beaten egg, and salt and pepper to taste into 4 cups hot mashed potatoes. Spoon into pastry bag with large star tip.

PLANTAIN (*plan' tin, -tuhn*)—**1.** A broad-leafed plant, the leaves of which are used in salads. **2.** A rather large, elongated, tropical fruit related to the banana, which it resembles closely in appearance.

Unlike the banana, however, this starchy fruit is unsuitable for eating raw. It is commonly baked, fried, or boiled. Crispy plantain chips are made by thinly slicing, then deep-fat frying this fruit. In South America where plantain is widely grown and in the Deep South, it is also enjoyed when cooked with hot peppers or a hot sauce.

Fried Plantains

Peel 2 ripe plantains (1 pound) with sharp knife. Cut in half crosswise, then in ¼-inch thick lengthwise pieces. Heat ¼ cup salad oil in skillet. Add plantain; fry till golden, about 6 to 8 minutes per side. Drain. Serves 4.

PLANTER'S PUNCH—A potent, dark rum and citrus juice beverage that was first created by Jamaican sugarcane planters.

Planter's Punch

> 1 tablespoon lime juice
> 1 teaspoon sugar
> 2 ounces Jamaica rum
> 1 teaspoon grenadine
>   Finely cracked ice
>   Club soda
> 1 maraschino cherry
> 1 stick fresh pineapple
> ½ orange slice

In a tall glass combine lime juice and sugar; stir till sugar is dissolved. Add rum and grenadine. Fill glass three-fourths full with ice; stir. Add club soda to taste. Trim with cherry, pineapple, and orange. Makes 1 drink.

PLASTIC—A material that is pliable at some time during its manufacture. Both heat and pressure are used to mold plastic into the desired shape.

Among other things, plastic is easy to care for, lightweight, less breakable than glass or ceramics, and not subject to rust. These advantages have made plastic particularly popular for kitchen utensils and dinnerware such as mixing bowls, refrigerator dishes, plates, and glasses.

PLATE—**1.** A very shallow piece of dinnerware used for serving food. **2.** The thin cut of beef between brisket and flank. It is a less-tender cut of meat, suitable for braising or for use in stews. (See also *Beef.*)

PLÄTTAR—The Swedish word for tiny, delicate pancakes often served as a dessert.

PLOVER (*pluv' uhr, plō' vuhr*)—A small, wild bird related to the sandpiper that is found in marshy areas. Both the plover meat and its eggs are valued in Europe.

PLUCK—**1.** To pull out the feathers of a bird, particularly domesticated poultry. **2.** The heart, liver, lungs, and other animal entrails that are eaten as food.

PLUM—A single-seeded fruit, member of the *Prunus* family, that is round to oval in shape, and has a smooth green, yellow, red, blue, or purple skin. When fully ripe, the thick, juicy fruit flesh is sweet to tangy, depending on the variety.

Plums are closely related to other stone or drupe fruits such as cherries, peaches, and apricots. The fruits are born on trees or shrubs that are grown not only for the edible fruits but often for the fragrant ornamental flowers and attractive foliage that are produced as well.

It is difficult to establish when and where the first plum trees grew since wild forms have been growing in both hemispheres for centuries. From the first plums, three main types of plums—European, Japanese, and American—developed in separate localities.

European plums originated in southwestern Asia around the Caucasus Mountain region, but cultivation quickly spread to other regions of Asia, and to Europe. Plum stones found at the Swiss lake dwellings indicate that Damson-type plums were being utilized some 5,000 years ago. (Damson plums are so old that they are named after the city of Damascus, Syria, where they have long been cultivated.) Assyrian writers, furthermore, recommended that plums be eaten with honey and butter. Greeks and Romans also ate plums, although there were apparently fewer plum varieties available than some other fruits. In any case, plums eaten fresh when in season and preserved during the winter months were a well-accepted food.

Nobody knows for sure just when the European plum was brought to America. It is known that the Spanish brought them to their southwestern missions, and that the French introduced plums in Canada. By 1775 Damson plums, now chiefly used for jellies, were the most widely cultivated variety in the United States.

Along front, plum varieties from left are El Capitan, Elephant Heart, Santa Rosa, Queen Ann, and Italian Prune. In back, from left are Ace, Kelsey, President, Mariposa, and El Dorado.

Japanese plums, the second varietal group, are actually indigenous to China. They were brought to Japan about 200 to 400 years ago. Japanese plums were introduced to the United States in 1870 by a Vacaville, California, fruit grower. Fortunately for today's consumers, the qualities of Japanese plums were recognized by the plant breeder, Luther Burbank.

An assortment of wild American plums seemingly thrived in every region of the United States when this country was first settled. Although not of good dessert quality, these plums made excellent preserves, jellies, and jams—a welcome addition to a sometimes bland diet. The Spanish explorer, DeSoto, who ventured up the Mississippi River in 1541, found Indians using plums like the Chickasaw variety, otherwise known as Indian cherries. New Englanders learned to utilize Canadian and beach plums that grew on coastal lands. As the western frontier was settled, the inhabitants made use of the wild plums indigenous to those regions.

How plums are produced: Although plum varieties gradually improved over the years, the most successful plum hybridization occurred during the latter part of the nineteenth and the early twentieth centuries. During 40 years of experimentation, Luther Burbank developed more than 60 plum and prune varieties, many of which are still commercially important. By crossing Japanese plums with European and American ones, fruits with excellent eating qualities were produced.

One reason for Burbank's success was his propagation technique—budding the desired plum varieties onto mature stock. Budding along with some grafting is still utilized today to perpetuate and improve the better varieties. Permanently planted when about two years old, the trees are continually cultivated in much the same way that apple and pear trees are grown.

Under certain conditions of moisture and humidity, plum trees are very susceptible to specific diseases and blights. Since climate is more easily controlled in dry regions that are irrigated, the western states, particularly California, Oregon, Washington, and Idaho have become the primary centers of plum production. Smaller commercial regions are found around the lake areas of Michigan and New York.

Nutritional value: Like other fruit, fresh and processed plums are packed with vital nutrients. One fresh 2-inch plum contains only 25 calories while contributing an assortment of vitamins and minerals including vitamins A and C, the B complex, iron, and calcium. One-half cup of plums canned in syrup provides 100 calories.

Types of plums: There are over 2000 varieties of European, Japanese, and American plums—stupefying to say the least. Most American varieties are sold locally and are not of commercial importance.

In general, there are certain characteristics that distinguish Japanese from European varieties. Japanese plums are usually medium to large in size; are juicy; have round or heart shapes; and are yellow to red or reddish orange in color. They never have blue or purple casts. Kelsey, Burbank, Wickson, Santa Rosa, and Satsuma are examples of Japanese varieties.

European plums, on the other hand, are generally smaller in size; have milder flavor and firmer texture; are oval or round in shape; and include blue and purple varieties as well as some with yellow, green, and red tones. The three best known varieties are the Italian prune, Damson, and Greengage plums.

The most unique European plums are prune plums, so named because they dry readily without fermenting. All prune plums are freestone (the pits separate readily from the flesh), in contrast to standard plums which are clingstones. The Italian prune plum is the best-known type but other varieties are also dried.

How to select and store: Although there are many more different plum varieties that are available in fresh form, the purchase of fresh plums is limited to the peak months of May through August. The homemaker of today, however, has canned and dried plums to choose from when the fresh plums are not in season. Commercially canned plums are usually the Italian variety, while those that are dried and sold as prunes include the d'Agen and Sugar Plum varieties.

As is true of some other fruits, plums do not continue to ripen after they are picked from the trees. This necessitates careful selection of fresh plums on the homemaker's part. The best buy are plums well colored for the variety, slightly soft to the touch, and free of decay.

To be avoided are the immature, overmature, and damaged fruit. Immature plums are very hard and will not soften or become juicy. Overmature plums are very soft, may leak juice, and show signs of decay or darkening of the flesh. Pass up sunburned plums with brownish red or brown marks on the skin, and fruit with cracks caused by poor growing conditions.

Once you've selected the choicest plums, be sure to store them right. Refrigerate plums, uncovered. Be sure to use them within three to five days.

How to use: To most people, plums are considered solely a snack or dessert fruit, yet even Little Jack Horner knew the merits of cooked plums when he tasted that Christmas pie. The stature of cooked plums gains as homemakers discover what a delectable flavor they add to cooked foods.

Besides their snack use, fresh plums are perfect for fruit cups served as the appetizer or dessert course, and for fruit salads as the side dish, main dish, or dessert. Use either halved or sliced plums as the situation dictates.

How to tell when plums are ripe

Did you see another unfamiliar plum variety at the grocery store recently and question whether the plums were ripe? It's little wonder with the large number of types available. The skin color guide below, which includes some of the most frequently marketed plums, will help you identify ripe fruit. Plums with slight softening and sound appearance are indicative of ripeness, too.

Varietal or group name	Ripe skin color
Beauty	Bright crimson
Burbank	Deep yellow overlaid with red; dotted with yellow spots
Formosa	Cherry red
Greengage	Green or yellow green
Italian Prune	Dark purple
Kelsey	Greenish bronze or reddish
President	Purple
Santa Rosa	Purplish crimson
Wickson	Yellowish red

Lemon-Frosted Plum Squares

A refreshing fruit trio—

Dissolve two 3-ounce packages strawberry-flavored gelatin and dash salt in 2½ cups boiling water; cool. Slowly add one 7-ounce bottle lemon-lime carbonated beverage and 2 tablespoons lemon juice. Chill till the mixture is partially set. Fold in 2 cups fresh, pitted plums cut in wedges. Pour into 8x8x2-inch pan; chill the mixture till *almost* firm.

Beat one 3¾-ounce package *instant* lemon pudding mix and 1¼ cups cold milk with electric mixer or rotary beater till smooth; add ½ cup dairy sour cream. Spread atop almost firm gelatin; chill till firm. Makes 6 to 8 servings.

Plums in a shell

A crunchy streusel topping adorns Crumb→ Top Plum Pie. The filling can be based on any of the richest plums of the season.

Plum Dessert Salad

      2 envelopes unflavored gelatin
          (2 tablespoons)
      1 cup sugar
      2 cups orange juice
      ¼ cup lemon juice
      2 cups fresh red plums, pitted
          and cut in wedges, *or* 17-
          ounce can purple plums, well
          drained and pitted
      Lemon Sauce

Combine gelatin and sugar; add 1½ cups cold water. Stir over low heat till gelatin and sugar are dissolved. Add orange and lemon juices. Chill till partially set. Set pan of gelatin in ice water; beat with rotary beater till light and foamy. Fold in plums. Pour into 6½-cup mold; chill till firm. Unmold; top salad with wreath of flaked coconut, if desired. Pass Lemon Sauce. Makes 8 servings.

Lemon Sauce: Beat 2 eggs and 1 tablespoon lemon juice together till thick and lemon-colored. Gradually add 1 cup sifted confectioners' sugar, beating constantly. Stir in ½ teaspoon vanilla, ¼ teaspoon grated lemon peel, and dash salt. Makes 1¾ cups.

The phrase "from soup to nuts" fits the many cooking uses for plums. Plum breads and coffee cakes are scrumptious. A plum sauce sparked with vinegar performs grandly as a meat sauce or glaze. If you add sugar to the plums instead of vinegar, the sauce is transformed into a topping for ice cream, cake, or parfaits. Other dessert creations that please those who delight in good home cooking include a variety of cobblers, pies, and cakes.

When there's an abundance of plums, preserve them by making plum jellies, jams, and butters. Your family will welcome these midwinter treats. (See *Fruit, Prune* for additional information.)

Coconut-wreathed mold

Plum Dessert Salad functions as a salad or as a dessert course. Be sure that fluffy Lemon Sauce is spooned over each serving.

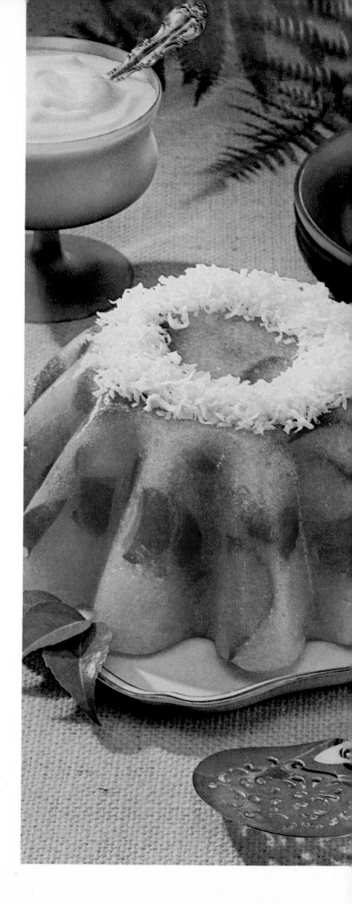

Plum Jewel Coffee Cake

Plums nestle under brown sugar topper—

>   2 cups sifted all-purpose flour
>   1/3 cup granulated sugar
>   3 teaspoons baking powder
>   1 teaspoon salt
>   1/3 cup shortening
>   2 slightly beaten eggs
>   1/2 cup milk
>   . . .
>   6 to 8 red plums, pitted and
>   sliced
>   2 tablespoons butter or margarine
>   1 cup brown sugar
>   1 1/2 teaspoons ground cinnamon

Sift together flour, granulated sugar, baking powder, and salt into mixing bowl. Cut in shortening till mixture resembles coarse meal. Combine eggs and milk; add to flour mixture, stirring just till dry ingredients are moistened. Turn into greased 11x7x1 1/2-inch baking pan, spreading dough evenly into corners.

Press plums into dough and dot with butter or margarine. Combine brown sugar and cinnamon; sprinkle over top. Bake at 375° for 20 to 25 minutes. Serve warm. Makes 8 or 9 servings.

Plum-Glazed Chicken

A background orange flavor pervades—

>   1 17-ounce can purple plums
>   1/4 teaspoon grated orange peel
>   1/4 cup orange juice
>   1/2 teaspoon ground cinnamon
>   1/2 teaspoon Worcestershire sauce
>   2 2 1/2- to 3-pound ready-to-cook
>   broiler-fryer chickens, cut up
>   Salad oil

Drain plums, reserving 3/4 cup syrup. Force plums through sieve; add plum syrup, orange peel and juice, cinnamon, and Worcestershire sauce. Mix ingredients very well.

Brush chicken pieces with salad oil. Season with salt and pepper. Cook chicken over *medium* coals 10 minutes; brush with glaze and continue cooking 15 minutes. Turn chicken; grill 20 minutes brushing with glaze the last 15 minutes of grilling. Makes 6 servings.

Crumb Top Plum Pie

>   1 3/4 pounds fresh plums,
>   pitted and quartered (4 1/2 cups)
>   1/3 cup water
>   3/4 to 1 cup sugar
>   3 tablespoons cornstarch
>   1/4 teaspoon salt
>   . . .
>   1 *unbaked* 9-inch pastry shell
>   (See *Pastry*)
>   1/3 cup sifted all-purpose flour
>   1/3 cup sugar
>   1/2 teaspoon ground cinnamon
>   1/4 teaspoon ground nutmeg
>   3 tablespoons butter or margarine

Combine plums and water; bring to boiling and cook 3 to 4 minutes. Mix 3/4 to 1 cup sugar to taste, cornstarch, and salt; stir into plum mixture. Cook slowly, stirring constantly, till thickened and clear, about 5 minutes. Remove from heat; cool. Turn into pastry shell. Combine flour, 1/3 cup sugar, cinnamon, and nutmeg. Cut in butter till crumbly. Sprinkle over top of pie. Bake at 400° for 30 to 35 minutes.

Italian Plum Cobbler

>   1 1/2 pounds Italian plums, pitted and
>   quartered (about 3 1/2 cups)
>   1 1/4 cups sugar
>   1/4 cup water
>   2 tablespoons quick-cooking
>   tapioca
>   2 tablespoons butter or margarine
>   . . .
>   1 1/2 cups packaged biscuit mix
>   2 tablespoons sugar
>   2 tablespoons butter or margarine,
>   melted
>   1/3 to 1/2 cup milk

Combine plums, 1 1/4 cups sugar, water, and tapioca. Cook over medium heat, stirring constantly, till mixture boils; stir in the 2 tablespoons butter. Pour into 8x8x2-inch pan.

Combine biscuit mix, 2 tablespoons sugar, and melted butter. Add enough milk to dry ingredients to moisten; drop by spoonfuls on top of hot plum mixture; spread atop. Bake at 425° till done, 20 minutes. Serve warm with plain or whipped cream, if desired. Serves 6 to 8.

Plums with Custard Sauce

Currant jelly and a dollop of meringue add a "floating island" twist to this dessert—

In a heavy saucepan beat together 2 egg yolks and 2 whole eggs; stir in ¼ cup sugar and ¼ teaspoon salt. Add 2 cups milk all at once. Cook and stir over medium heat till mixture coats a metal spoon. Remove pan from heat; place pan in sink or bowl of cold water. Stir custard a minute or two to hasten cooling, then add ½ teaspoon vanilla.

Drain and pit one 17-ounce can plums; quarter plums. Divide evenly between 6 sherbet dishes. Spoon cooled custard sauce over. Beat 2 egg whites till soft peaks form; gradually beat in ¼ cup sugar till stiff peaks form. Spoon a dollop of meringue over each serving of fruit and custard. Garnish with a spoonful of currant jelly. Makes 6 servings.

PLUMP—**1.** A word used to describe food, especially fruit, that has a full, round shape in contrast to a shriveled one. **2.** To allow a food, such as dried fruit, to swell and soften by soaking in water.

PLUM PUDDING—A steamed pudding consisting of suet, fruits, nuts, flour, eggs, and spices. English in origin, plum pudding is traditionally prepared for holiday eating and, thus, is also called Christmas pudding. Frequently served as a liquor-flamed masterpiece, plum pudding is accompanied by a butter- and sugar-based sauce.

The development of plum pudding goes back to very early times. The idea evolved from a thick, boiled porridge to which plums were added. The first published recipe appeared in 1675, and by 1700 raisins had replaced the plums, although the dish retained its "plum" name. Today, raisins and other dried or candied fruit are used in place of the plums.

In the English style

←'Tis the season for Regal Plum Pudding, decked with a sprig of holly and red candied cherries, then served with Hard Sauce.

Old-fashioned plum pudding is steamed as the holiday meat roasts or made ahead and stored in a cool, dry place for several weeks. To reheat before serving, steam for an hour, or heat the unmolded pudding the same amount of time in the top of a double boiler over boiling water. (See *Christmas, English Cookery, Pudding* for additional information.)

Regal Plum Pudding

      4 slices bread, torn up
      1 cup milk
      2 slightly beaten eggs
      1 cup brown sugar
     ¼ cup orange juice
      6 ounces beef suet, ground
         (2 cups)
      1 teaspoon vanilla
               • • •
      1 cup sifted all-purpose flour
      1 teaspoon baking soda
     ½ teaspoon salt
      2 teaspoons ground cinnamon
      1 teaspoon ground cloves
      1 teaspoon ground mace
               • • •
      2 cups raisins
      1 cup snipped, pitted dates
     ½ cup chopped mixed candied
         fruits and peels
     ½ cup chopped walnuts
         Hard Sauce

Soak bread in milk; beat. Stir in eggs, brown sugar, orange juice, beef suet, and vanilla. Sift together flour, baking soda, salt, cinnamon, cloves, and mace. Add raisins, dates, fruits and peels, and walnuts; mix well. Stir in bread mixture. Pour into well-greased 8½-cup mold. Cover the mixture with aluminum foil; tie the foil with a piece of string.

Place on rack in deep kettle; add boiling water, 1 inch deep. Cover; steam 3½ hours, adding water if needed. Cool 10 minutes; unmold. Stud with candied cherries, if desired. Serve warm with Hard Sauce. Serves 13.

Hard Sauce: Thoroughly cream together ½ cup butter or margarine and 2 cups sifted confectioners' sugar. Add 1 teaspoon vanilla. Spread the mixture in 8x8x2-inch pan; chill sauce to harden it. Cut in squares.

Easy Plum Pudding

This modernized adaptation breaks tradition since it's baked and contains plums—

    ½ **cup butter or margarine**
    2 **cups sifted confectioners'**
        sugar
    1 **beaten egg yolk**
    1 **teaspoon vanilla**
    1 **stiff-beaten egg white**

        •   •   •

    1 **17-ounce can purple plums**
    1 **package gingerbread mix**
    ½ **teaspoon salt**
    1 **cup light raisins**
    ½ **cup chopped walnuts**

        •   •   •

    ¼ **cup granulated sugar**
    2 **tablespoons cornstarch**
    1 **tablespoon lemon juice**

Prepare hard sauce by thoroughly creaming together butter and confectioners' sugar. Stir in egg yolk and vanilla. Fold in egg white. Chill the sauce thoroughly.

Drain plums, reserving syrup for sauce. Remove pits and cut plums in pieces. Prepare gingerbread mix according to package directions, adding plum pieces and salt to batter. Stir in light raisins and walnuts. Turn batter into well-greased 6½-cup mold.* Bake, uncovered, at 375° about 1 hour. Loosen edges of pudding from mold and immediately unmold onto plate.

To poach an egg, slip the egg into a pan of swirling, simmering water as you follow the direction of the swirl with the saucedish.

Meanwhile, prepare plum sauce by adding water to reserved plum syrup to make 1½ cups. Combine sugar and cornstarch in small saucepan. Gradually stir in plum syrup. Cook over medium heat, stirring constantly, till mixture is thickened and bubbly. Cook and stir 1 minute more. Stir in lemon juice. Serve plum sauce over pudding; pass hard sauce. Serves 10 to 12.

*Or, pour batter into 12 well-greased 5-ounce custard cups. Arrange cups in large shallow baking pan. Cover each cup with foil and bake at 375° for about 40 minutes.

PLUNGE—To immerse or submerge a solid food into a liquid. To blanch vegetables for freezing, the vegetables are plunged into boiling water for a specified time.

POACH—To cook a food in simmering (not boiling) liquid until the food is done, but still firm enough to hold its shape. Eggs are poached in water, milk, or tomato juice. Poaching fish in seasoned water or in a court bouillon adds an especially delicate flavor. When a food such as chicken is poached in butter, it is simply sautéed.

POD—The outer covering of a seed vegetable such as beans and legumes. For most podded vegetables, the pod is removed and only the seeds are eaten. Some exceptions to this are snap beans and the mini-seeded Chinese pea pods.

POI *(poi, pō' ē)*—A gray, starchy, porridge-like paste made by pounding and kneading cooked taro root. Native to Pacific islands, poi is eaten by itself or as an accompaniment to meat or fish. When freshly made, poi has a very bland taste; when allowed to ferment for two or three days, it develops a mildly acidic flavor.

Water is mixed with poi to adjust the consistency. Three thicknesses, which are described by the number of fingers needed to eat poi, are common. One-finger poi is thick enough so that the forefinger alone can scoop up a mouthful. Two-finger poi is somewhat thinner than one-finger poi, while three-finger poi is the thinnest type of poi and can only be dipped satisfactorily if three fingers are held tightly together. (See also *Hawaiian Cookery*.)

POKEWEED—A tall, sturdy, wild plant, part of which is eaten as a springtime green. When the young, greenish red stalks are a few inches high, they are cut off and cooked like asparagus. Care must be taken not to include the purple berries or roots since both plant parts are poisonous.

POLAND WATER—A bottled mineral water containing carbonic acid. This mineral water is named after the town in which it is produced, Poland Springs, Maine.

POLENTA—An Italian mush or porridge made by boiling a cornmeal or farina mixture in water. Polenta is served as a bread substitute or as a vegetable and is usually served with Parmesan cheese and/or a tomato sauce. It is eaten in its thick porridge state, or is molded, then sliced and sautéed in oil. (See also *Italian Cookery*.)

Tomato Polenta

Quick version using corn muffin mix—

½ cup finely chopped onion
1 clove garlic, minced
2 tablespoons salad oil
1 16-ounce can tomatoes, cut up
1 8-ounce can tomato sauce
1 3-ounce can chopped mushrooms, undrained
1 8-ounce package brown-and-serve sausage links, cut crosswise
½ teaspoon dried oregano leaves, crushed
¼ teaspoon salt
Dash pepper

• • •

½ cup grated Parmesan cheese
1 8-ounce package corn muffin mix
2 ounces sharp process American cheese, shredded (½ cup)

In skillet cook onion and garlic in hot oil just till tender. Add next 7 ingredients; simmer, uncovered, 5 minutes. Add Parmesan cheese to muffin mix. Prepare muffin mix according to package directions; spread in greased 8x8x2-inch baking dish. Top with tomato mixture. Bake at 400° for 30 minutes. Sprinkle with American cheese. Makes 5 to 6 servings.

Italian Polenta

The cornmeal mixture in this recipe is prepared in the conventional way—

2½ cups water
1½ cups yellow cornmeal
1½ cups cold water
1½ teaspoons salt
¼ cup butter or margarine

• • •

½ pound ground beef
2 tablespoons chopped onion
½ clove garlic, crushed

• • •

⅓ cup water
1 16-ounce can tomatoes, cut up
1 8-ounce can tomato sauce
1 3-ounce can sliced mushrooms, undrained
2 tablespoons snipped parsley
½ teaspoon dried oregano leaves, crushed
¼ teaspoon salt
¼ teaspoon dried thyme leaves, crushed
1 small bay leaf

• • •

Grated Parmesan cheese

In saucepan bring the 2½ cups water to boiling. Combine yellow cornmeal, cold water, and salt. Stir into boiling water. Cook, stirring constantly, till thick. Cover; cook over very low heat about 45 minutes, stirring occasionally. Spread in 8x8x2-inch baking pan. Cool thoroughly. Cut into 6 pieces. In skillet brown polenta squares in butter till golden, about 5 to 6 minutes per side. Meanwhile, in large saucepan cook ground beef with chopped onion and crushed garlic till meat is brown. Drain off excess fat. Add the ⅓ cup water, tomatoes, tomato sauce, mushrooms, snipped parsley, oregano, salt, thyme, and bay leaf. Bring mixture to boiling; reduce heat. Simmer, uncovered, till thick, about 1¼ hours. Stir the sauce occasionally. Remove the bay leaf. Serve tomato sauce over the polenta squares. Pass Parmesan cheese. Serves 6.

POLISH HAM—A canned, cured and smoked ham imported from Poland. Polish ham has a distinctive, strong flavor that appeals to many people. (See also *Ham*.)

POLISH SAUSAGE—A garlic-flavored sausage containing both ground beef and pork. The links are smoked and may be fully cooked. (See also *Sausage*.)

POLLACK, POLLOCK (*pol' uhk*)—A saltwater fish, also known as Boston bluefish, found in northern Atlantic waters. Pollack is related to cod and haddock, and like these two fish, it has firm, white flesh with a delicate flavor. Pollack has greenish coloring which becomes yellowish or gray on the sides and silvery gray on the underside. A light line along the side of the body identifies this fish. Pollack weigh from 3 to 14 pounds and measure 2 to 3 feet long.

The supply of pollack is increasing in United States markets. These fish are becoming more popular and are being used in place of haddock, which have become more scarce. Pollack are sold mainly as fresh or frozen fillets. Some drawn, dressed, and smoked fish are available, too.

Pollack are lean fish and can be steamed, boiled, or fried. They can be baked or broiled if melted butter or oil is added.

When eaten, pollack supply protein, minerals, and B vitamins to the diet. A 3½-ounce serving contains 95 calories before cooking. (See also *Fish*.)

POLONAISE, À LA (*pol' uh nāz', pō' luh-*)—A garnish consisting of butter, dry bread crumbs, and sometimes chopped hard-cooked egg yolk and snipped parsley that is used on vegetables. Literally, this French phrase means "in the Polish style." This pretty and flavorful garnish is particularly suitable as a topping on cooked Brussels sprouts, broccoli, and cauliflower.

POLYNESIAN COOKERY (*pol' uh nē' zhuhn*)—The cooking traditions developed by the ancestral people living on widely scattered island groups in the Pacific Ocean. Among these islands are Tonga, Fiji, Tahiti, Samoa, and the Hawaiian, Marshall, Gilbert, and Caroline islands.

Through the years, the cuisines of some of these islands have been exposed to outside cultures. Thus, some French-style cooking has been incorporated into the Polynesian cooking of Tahiti, and Hawaiian cooking is a mixture of oriental, Polynesian, American, and European styles. Elsewhere, the traditional island cookery continues, little changed from the original. (See also *Hawaiian Cookery*.)

POME (*pōm*)—Any fruit with a seeded core surrounded by juicy flesh. Apples and pears are examples of pome fruit.

POMEGRANATE (*pom' gran' it, pom' uh-*)—A tropical, subtly angulated fruit with a yellow to red or purple red skin and a short neck. In size, the pomegranate is comparable to a large apple or orange. The leathery skin is enclosed in a papery red, pink, or white pulp in which a mass of juicy, crimson seeds is embedded. The edible seeds, pulp, and juice have a slightly sweet, yet tangy flavor.

In the ancient civilizations, pomegranates were known from the eastern Mediterranean countries all the way to India. These fruits were an important source of food to these people.

Most likely native to Iran, pomegranates were highly regarded by Assyrians, Hittites, Persians, and Egyptians. Ancient Assyrian monuments are adorned with pomegranate figures; similar drawings were used on the tombs of Egyptian kings.

Tests and remains of the early civilizations included in Biblical history have also alluded to pomegranate use. They are referred to in the *Holy Bible* by the Israelites who longed for the fruit as they traveled through the wilderness. In later times, King Solomon had pomegranate orchards. And carbonized remains of pomegranates have been found where the town of Jericho once stood.

Pomegranates' symbolic pertinence has spanned the globe. They have been a fertility symbol in China, Persia, Greece, and Rome because the fruits contain so many seeds. Chinese women have offered pomegranates to their goddess of mercy in efforts to have sons in preference to daughters. In Turkey, brides have broken pomegranates on the ground. The number of seeds that scattered would equal the number of children she would bear. In Greece, pomegranates have been called the "fruit of Hades," a reference influenced by Greek mythology. And to Christians throughout

Often called "the apple with many seeds," the pomegranate is a colorful autumn-winter fruit with sweet, yet tangy flavor.

the world, pomegranates have been an artistic symbol of hope.

The American heritage of pomegranates indicates that the first fruits were brought to Mexico and California by the Spanish. Today, California remains the primary area of production in the United States.

Nutritional value: The juiciness of pomegranates reflects their high water content. The pulp and seeds of 1 medium pomegranate contains 63 calories. The presence of vitamins and minerals is less significant.

How to select and store: Two-thirds of these autumn fruits are marketed in October, although a fair number are available in September and November. Choose pomegranates that are thin-skinned, bright purple red in color, and fresh.

When kept out of direct sunlight, they will stay fresh a few days at room temperature. If refrigerated, the fruit can be stored somewhat longer.

How to prepare and use: Although the juice and seeds of pomegranates are most frequently utilized, the pulp is edible, too. Halve the pomegranate, then use a fork (for stain-free fingers) to push out the seeds. Eat the pulp as is or squeeze out the juice and use it for a beverage.

Pomegranate seeds add brilliant color, flavor, and texture to fruit salads and desserts. Pomegranate juice is a pleasant addition to fruit punches and drinks. It is sometimes the basis for the commercial product, grenadine syrup, used in alcoholic cocktails. (See also *Fruit.*)

Holiday Cocktail Deluxe

4 white grapefruit, sectioned
⅓ cup pomegranate seeds
1 tablespoon grenadine syrup
1 cup low-calorie lemon-lime
   carbonated beverage, chilled

In bowl combine grapefruit sections, pomegranate seeds, and grenadine syrup. Chill at least 30 minutes, stirring once or twice.

To serve, spoon fruit and syrup into sherbet dishes. Slowly pour lemon-lime carbonated beverage over fruit mixture. Makes 8 servings.

Holiday Turkey Salad

Studded with pomegranate seeds—

2 cups cubed cooked turkey
1 cup sliced celery
1 8¾-ounce can pineapple
   tidbits, drained (⅔ cup)
½ cup pomegranate seeds
½ cup mayonnaise or salad
   dressing
¼ cup toasted slivered almonds

Combine all ingredients; toss. Chill. Serve on lettuce-lined plates. Serves 4 or 5.

POMELO *(pom' uh lō)* — **1.** Another name for the shaddock, ancestor of today's grapefruit. **2.** An alternate name for grapefruit. (See also *Grapefruit.*)

POMME *(pôm)* — The French word for apple. Confusion arises when the French term for potatoes, *pommes de terre* (apples of the earth), is shortened to *pommes.*

POMME DE TERRE (*pom duh târ'*)—The French word for potato. Literally, the phrase means "apple of the earth."

POMPANO (*pom' puh nō'*)—A fat, saltwater fish. Pompano live along the Gulf coast, the Atlantic coast from Cape Cod to Brazil, and a few live on the Pacific coast. These fish, relatives of the mackerels, have deep bodies with blue, silver, or golden coloring. The length averages about 18 inches and weight, 1½ pounds. The flesh has a rich, yet delicate flavor.

The nutritional value of pompano consists of proteins, minerals, and the B vitamins. An uncooked piece measuring 3x3x ¾ inches contains 166 calories.

Pompano are available all year, both fresh and frozen. These whole fish or fillets can be baked, broiled, fried, boiled, or steamed. One of the more famous recipes is Pompano En Papillote in which the fish and the sauce are baked inside a parchment bag. (See also *Fish*.)

Pompano with Dill Sauce

      2 pounds fresh or frozen pompano
          fillets
      2 cups boiling water
      2 tablespoons lemon juice
      1 clove garlic, minced
      1 teaspoon salt
      3 egg yolks
      2 tablespoons lemon juice
    ¼ teaspoon dried dillweed
    ½ cup butter

Thaw frozen fish; cut fish into 6 portions. Place in a greased skillet. Add the boiling water, 2 tablespoons lemon juice, minced garlic, and salt. Cover; simmer till fish flakes easily when tested with a fork, 5 to 10 minutes.

Meanwhile, place egg yolks, 2 tablespoons lemon juice, and dillweed in blender container. Cover; quickly turn blender on and off.

Heat butter till melted and almost boiling. Turn blender on high speed. Slowly pour in butter, blending till thick and fluffy, about 30 seconds. Hold over warm, *not hot*, water till ready to serve. Carefully remove fish to platter; pour some hot sauce over fish. Pass remaining sauce. Makes 6 servings.

Pompano Amandine

    1½ pounds fresh or frozen pompano
          fillets
      2 tablespoons butter, melted
      1 tablespoon lemon juice
    ¾ teaspoon salt
          Dash pepper
      1 tablespoon butter
    ¼ cup sliced almonds
      1 tablespoon lemon juice
      2 teaspoons snipped parsley

Thaw frozen fish; cut fish fillets into 4 portions. Place in greased baking pan. Combine 2 tablespoons melted butter and 1 tablespoon lemon juice. Brush on fish. Sprinkle with the salt and pepper. Bake, uncovered, at 350° till fish flakes easily when tested with a fork, 20 minutes.

Melt 1 tablespoon butter in skillet. Brown almonds in butter till golden, stirring constantly. Remove nuts; sprinkle over fish. Stir 1 tablespoon lemon juice and snipped parsley into melted butter remaining in skillet. Heat. Drizzle over fish. Makes 6 servings.

PONE—Another name for the southern favorite, corn pone. (See also *Corn Pone*.)

PONY—1. A small glass used for liquor. 2. The amount of liquid this glass holds, usually about one ounce.

POOR BOY SANDWICH—A sandwich made by filling a half loaf of French bread, horizontally sliced, with assorted meats and cheeses, lettuce, and relish.

First made in New Orleans during the Depression years, the poor boy sandwich was developed as an inexpensive, yet hearty lunch that the working man could buy. It was patterned after the more costly French bread sandwich (a loaf of French bread filled with roast beef or ham). To make the "po' boy," the loaf of bread was made thinner, and less expensive ingredients were used for the filling of the sandwich. (See also *Sandwich*.)

POP—1. To heat grain kernels until they explode, as when popping corn. 2. Name for a flavored, carbonated nonalcoholic beverage. (See also *Carbonated Beverage*.)

POPCORN—A special type of dried corn that, when cooked, explodes into fluffy puffs many times its original size. The popcorn kernel has a flinty starch exterior with a little soft starch near the center. When heated, the moisture inside the kernel becomes steam. The "pop" is many tiny explosions as each starch grain expands and bursts its armor of hard starch.

Varieties of popcorn are based on kernel shape, either pearl (short and thick) or rice (with pointed crown). It is further classified by color—yellow or white.

Popcorn was eaten by early European explorers. Columbus found West Indians wearing it as ornaments; Cortez came across it in Mexico in 1519. Today, popcorn is a very popular snack.

To store, keep kernels in a tightly covered container once the package has been opened, or refrigerate. This helps retain the bit of moisture in the kernels.

Traditionally, popcorn, the favorite movie-theater snack, is tossed with melted butter and salt. Other popular concoctions are the caramelized sugar-popcorn mixtures for caramel corn and popcorn balls.

Popcorn

Follow manufacturer's directions if using an electric corn popper, or heat regular popcorn popper or heavy medium skillet just till warm. Add ¼ cup cooking oil or shortening (omit cooking oil or shortening if using an old-fashioned wire popper over coals). Heat over medium-high heat till hot, about 2 to 3 minutes.

Drop in 3 or 4 kernels of popcorn. When these begin to spin and pop, add ½ cup popcorn. Reduce heat to medium-low. Cover the popper or skillet and shake it gently.

When popping stops, remove pan from heat and empty the popped corn into a large bowl. Add melted butter or margarine and salt to taste. Serve immediately if possible.

Parmesan Popcorn

Mix 1 quart hot popped corn with 2 tablespoons butter or margarine and ½ teaspoon seasoned salt. Toss with ¼ cup shredded Parmesan cheese. Float the popcorn atop soup.

Pastel Popcorn Tree is made of popcorn ball "branches" decorated with pink marshmallows. Top with candy canes and a red bow.

Popcorn Pops

    4 quarts popped corn (⅔ cup
        unpopped)
    1 cup peanuts
    1 cup light molasses
    1 cup granulated sugar
    1 teaspoon salt

Combine popped corn and peanuts in a large bowl or in a pan. In a 2-quart saucepan, combine molasses, sugar, and salt; cook over medium heat to hard-ball stage (250°). Pour syrup slowly over the popped corn and nuts, stirring till the mixture is well coated with syrup. Press into 5-ounce cold-drink cups. Insert a wooden skewer in each; let cool. Push on the bottoms of cups to remove. Makes 16.

Caramel Popcorn Balls

    ¼ cup butter or margarine
    1 cup brown sugar
    ½ cup light corn syrup
            • • •
    ½ 15-ounce can sweetened
        condensed milk (⅔ cup)
    ½ teaspoon vanilla
    5 quarts popped corn

In saucepan, combine butter, sugar, and corn syrup. Stir well and bring to boiling over medium heat. Stir in condensed milk; simmer, stirring constantly, till mixture comes to soft-ball stage (234° to 238°). Stir in vanilla. Pour over popped corn and stir to coat. Butter hands lightly; shape popcorn into balls about 3½ inches in diameter. Makes about 15.

Candied Popcorn

Tint yellow or green next time—

    2½ quarts popped corn
    1 cup granulated sugar
    1 cup water
    8 drops red food coloring
    1 teaspoon vanilla
    2 tablespoons confectioners'
        sugar

Place popped corn in large greased bowl. In small saucepan combine granulated sugar and water. Cook and stir over low heat till sugar dissolves. Continue cooking, without stirring, to soft-ball stage (238°). Stir in food coloring and vanilla. Pour syrup over popcorn, tossing to coat. Sprinkle with confectioners' sugar; mix to separate kernels.

Pastel Popcorn Tree

White Popcorn Balls

    5 quarts popped corn (about 2 cups
        unpopped)
    2 cups sugar
    ½ teaspoon salt
    1½ cups water
    ½ cup light corn syrup
    1 teaspoon vinegar
    1 teaspoon vanilla

Keep popcorn hot and crisp in 300° to 325° oven. Butter sides of saucepan. In it, combine sugar, salt, water, syrup, and vinegar. Cook to hard-ball stage (250°). Stir in vanilla. Pour cooked syrup slowly over hot popped corn, stirring just enough to combine the ingredients thoroughly. Butter hands and shape the popcorn mixture into 2-inch balls.

Pink Popcorn Balls

Prepare as for white popcorn balls above *except* omit vinegar (to ensure pretty pink color) and vanilla. Add ¼ teaspoon red food coloring and ¼ teaspoon peppermint extract to cooked syrup. Shape some of the red popcorn mixture into 11 balls 2½ inches in diameter, the remainder into 2-inch balls.

Marshmallow Sparkles

        Red food coloring
    ½ 3-ounce package strawberry- or
        raspberry-flavored gelatin
        Marshmallows, large and miniature

Add food coloring, a few drops at a time, to gelatin, mixing well to obtain desired color. (A blender does the trick beautifully.) Dip a few marshmallows by hand into water. Drain excess moisture by shaking in paper toweling. Roll marshmallows in colored gelatin and allow to dry thoroughly.

To *assemble tree:* On flat plate or tray, arrange a circle of the eleven 2½-inch pink balls, securing one to the other with toothpicks. Fill in center with 7 white balls. Pyramid remaining balls, alternating colors; continue to fill in centers with white balls. If desired, omit top ball and carefully insert 3 large candy canes tied with a red bow. Tuck in Marshmallow Sparkles.

POPOVER—A big, puffy, steam-raised quick bread with a crusty outer shell and a hollow interior. The crisp, golden brown shell has a tender, moist lining.

Before the advent of a reliable baking powder in the mid-1800s, popovers were one of the few quick bread alternatives the homemaker had to the time-consuming yeast-raised breads. It seems likely that the name popover came about because the batter "popped over" the edge of the pan in which it was baked. In fact, cast iron pans resembling muffin pans, but with straighter sides, were manufactured specifically as popover pans.

The Englishman's beloved Yorkshire pudding is actually popover batter made with drippings from roast beef and baked in a large pan rather than as individual popovers. The popover is also a first cousin of the cream puff, as they both contain the same basic ingredients, only in different proportions. Popover batter is quite thin; cream puff dough is very stiff. Both are leavened by the steam that forms during the first few minutes of baking at a very high temperature. However, the steam would be useless if it were not for the physical properties of the ingredients used in popovers, particularly those of the flour and of the whole eggs.

When making popovers, all-purpose flour or bread flour is essential because it contains a large amount of hard-wheat protein, which forms gluten when mixed with a liquid. As the batter is beaten, the gluten develops an elastic quality that later allows the gluten to stretch to form the shell around the expanding steam. (Do not use cake flour since the gluten-producing protein, unnecessary in cake baking, is present in only a very small amount.) At the same time the gluten is stretching, the starch in the flour swells to produce the moist, tender lining.

The amount of egg in popovers has a great effect on the final volume. Two eggs per cup of flour is the standard proportion, but three eggs are sometimes used. The beaten egg stretches along with the starch during the high temperature baking, then it begins to coagulate so that the walls of the shell will not collapse before baking of the popover is completed.

Other ingredients are also important in popovers. Milk is the liquid and salt adds flavor. Although popovers could be made without shortening or oil, these ingredients contribute greatly to the tenderness of the final popover product.

In years gone by, two steps were considered important in making popovers—although neither is now necessary. One was lengthy beating. The other was preheating the popover pan or custard cups before pouring in the batter. Test kitchen experience has shown that you need not beat the batter for more than two minutes, pro-

Add the amount of curry to suit your taste for Curried Ham in Popovers. Then, spoon the flavorful meat mixture over Popovers.

Serve crisp and crusty Popovers hot from the oven. For elegant entertaining, accompany with butter curls and sweet-tart jelly.

viding the beating is done with a rotary beater or an electric mixer. Beating is even easier and quicker with a blender. And since there is no appreciable difference between popovers from preheated pans and those from pans not preheated, you do not have to preheat the pan or cups.

As the popovers complete the last few minutes of baking, prick them with a fork to prevent sogginess. Since the structure of the popovers has already been set, the popovers will not collapse when this is done. Then, when the baking time is up, if you prefer dry, crisp popovers, turn off the oven and leave them in the oven 30 minutes longer with the oven door ajar.

Popovers are easy to make and a delight to serve. In addition to being crusty and delicious, they are bound to generate conversation. Popovers are equally at home with butter and jam for breakfast or as a piping-hot partner for a luncheon salad or a bowl of soup. Split lengthwise, popovers steal the spotlight when the hollow is filled with a creamed mixture. And who can pass them by when they are served with a beef dinner. (See also *Bread.*)

A few minutes before baking time is up, prick Popovers with a fork to let the steam escape. This helps to make Popovers crisp.

Toasted with butter and Parmesan cheese, Poppy Seed Rolls are easy-to-fix grillmates for steak or chicken cooked over the coals.

Popovers

    2 eggs
    1 cup milk
    1 cup sifted all–purpose flour
    ½ teaspoon salt
    1 tablespoon salad oil

Place eggs in mixing bowl; add milk, flour, and salt. Beat 1½ minutes with rotary or electric beater. Add oil and beat 30 seconds longer. Pour batter into 6 to 8 greased custard cups, filling them only half full.

Bake at 475° for 15 minutes. Reduce oven temperature to 350° and bake till browned and firm, 25 to 30 minutes longer. (Do not open oven door to peek until total baking time is almost completed.) A few minutes before removing from oven, prick with a fork to let the steam escape. Serve hot. Makes 6 to 8 popovers.

Note: If you like popovers dry and crisp, turn off oven after popovers are baked and leave them in oven 30 minutes with oven door ajar.

Pecan Popovers

Follow recipe for Popovers. Stir ¼ cup finely chopped pecans into batter before filling the custard cups. Bake as directed above.

Curried Ham in Popovers

    2 tablespoons chopped green
        pepper
    1 tablespoon chopped onion
    1 tablespoon butter or margarine

        • • •

    1 10½-ounce can condensed cream
        of celery soup
    ⅓ cup mayonnaise or salad
        dressing
    ⅓ cup milk
    ¼ to ½ teaspoon curry powder
    2 cups cubed fully cooked ham
    6 popovers

In medium saucepan cook green pepper and onion in butter or margarine till tender but not brown. Stir in celery soup, mayonnaise or salad dressing, milk, curry powder, and cubed ham. Cook and stir till heated through. Split hot popovers lengthwise. Spoon creamed ham mixture into popover halves. Makes 6 servings.

POPPY SEED—The tiny, slate blue seeds of an annual poppy plant. Poppy seeds are so small that it takes about 900,000 to make a pound. Although they appear to be round, these tiny seeds are actually kidney-shaped.

Although the poppy from which poppy seeds come is thought to be native to Asia, most of the seeds imported today come from Holland. Some come from France, Poland, Germany, and England, too. These seeds come from the same poppy plant that gives opium; however, because of the plant structure, the ripe, dried seeds have no narcotic properties and are perfectly safe to eat as a food.

Poppy seeds have been enjoyed as a food for hundreds of years in Greece, India, and Europe. And they are still in wide use today. Occasionally, the seeds are crushed for the oil that they contain, which is used in the production of some margarines. Most often, however, poppy seeds are used as toppers for breads, mixed with noodles, or ground or crushed and sweetened for use as filling for rolls, sweet breads, and desserts. When the seeds are toasted, the nutty flavor is enhanced, as the heat brings out the flavor of the oil. Because of their oil content, poppy seeds that are not used right away should be stored in the refrigerator to prevent rancidity from developing at a rapid rate.

In addition to the whole seeds, prepared poppy seed fillings are available on the market. These fillings are ready to use in cakes, coffee cakes, and sweet breads.

Poppy Seed-Lime Dressing

$\frac{1}{3}$ cup vinegar
$\frac{1}{4}$ cup lime juice
. . .
$\frac{3}{4}$ cup sugar
1 teaspoon salt
1 teaspoon dry mustard
1 teaspoon poppy seed
1 teaspoon paprika
1 cup salad oil
$\frac{1}{2}$ teaspoon onion juice

In saucepan heat vinegar and lime juice to boiling. Combine sugar, salt, dry mustard, poppy seed, and paprika. Add to hot mixture in saucepan. Stir to dissolve sugar. Add salad oil and onion juice. Beat with rotary beater till thoroughly mixed and slightly thickened. Chill thoroughly. Spoon the salad dressing over fresh or canned fruit. Makes $1\frac{3}{4}$ cups dressing.

Stroganoff with Poppy Seed Noodles

1 pound beef sirloin, cut in $\frac{1}{4}$-inch strips
1 tablespoon shortening or oil
1 medium onion, sliced
1 clove garlic, crushed
1 $10\frac{1}{2}$-ounce can condensed cream of mushroom soup
1 cup dairy sour cream
1 3-ounce can broiled sliced mushrooms, undrained ($\frac{2}{3}$ cup)
2 tablespoons catsup
2 teaspoons Worcestershire sauce
4 ounces medium noodles, cooked
1 tablespoon butter or margarine
1 teaspoon poppy seed

In skillet brown meat in hot shortening. Add onion and garlic; cook till onion is crisp-tender. Blend next 5 ingredients. Pour over meat. Cook and stir over low heat till hot. Drain noodles; toss with butter and poppy seed. Serve sauce over noodles. Makes 4 servings.

Poppy Seed Torte

$\frac{1}{3}$ cup poppy seed
$\frac{3}{4}$ cup milk
$\frac{3}{4}$ cup butter or margarine
$1\frac{1}{2}$ cups sugar
$1\frac{1}{2}$ teaspoons vanilla
2 cups sifted cake flour
$2\frac{1}{2}$ teaspoons baking powder
$\frac{1}{4}$ teaspoon salt
4 stiffly beaten egg whites
Filling

Soak poppy seed in milk for 1 hour. Cream butter and sugar till fluffy. Mix in vanilla and milk with seed. Sift together dry ingredients; stir into creamed mixture. Fold in egg whites. Bake in 2 well-greased and lightly floured $8x1\frac{1}{2}$-inch round pans at 375° till cake tests done, about 20 to 25 minutes. Cool 10 minutes; remove from pans. Cool. Split layers. Spread Filling between layers; chill. Sift confectioners' sugar atop the torte.

Filling: In saucepan mix $\frac{1}{2}$ cup sugar and 1 tablespoon cornstarch. Combine $1\frac{1}{2}$ cups milk and 4 slightly beaten egg yolks. Stir into sugar. Cook and stir till bubbly; cool. Add 1 teaspoon vanilla and $\frac{1}{4}$ cup chopped walnuts.

Poppy Seed Swirled Bread

    2 packages active dry yeast
    5 to 6 cups sifted all-purpose
        flour
    1½ cups milk
    ⅓ cup sugar
    ⅓ cup shortening
    1 teaspoon salt
    3 eggs
        Poppy Seed Filling

In large mixer bowl combine yeast with *2 cups* of the flour. Heat together milk, sugar, shortening, and salt just till warm, stirring to melt shortening. Add to dry ingredients. Add eggs. Beat at low speed ½ minute, scraping bowl constantly. Beat 3 minutes at high speed. By hand, stir in enough of the remaining flour to make a moderately stiff dough.

Turn out onto lightly floured surface; knead till smooth and satiny, 5 to 10 minutes. Shape into ball. Place in lightly greased bowl, turning once to grease surface. Cover; let rise in warm place till double, 1 to 1¾ hours.

Meanwhile, prepare *Poppy Seed Filling:* Pour 1 cup boiling water over ¾ cup poppy seed (4 ounces); drain. Cover with 1 cup lukewarm water and let stand 30 minutes. Drain thoroughly. Grind the poppy seed in blender, or use the finest blade of food grinder. Stir in ½ cup chopped nuts, ⅓ cup honey, and 1 teaspoon grated lemon peel. Fold in 1 stiffly beaten egg white.

Punch down bread dough. Divide dough in 2 parts. Cover and let rest 10 minutes. On lightly floured board, roll one part of dough to a 24x 8-inch rectangle; spread with *half* the filling. Roll up, starting on 8-inch side; seal long ends. Place, seam side down, in greased 9x5x3-inch loaf pan. Repeat with second part of dough and filling. Cover loaves with cloth. Let rise till double, 30 to 45 minutes. Bake at 350° for 35 to 40 minutes. Remove from pans and cool on rack. Makes 2 loaves.

Poppy Seed Rolls

    3 tablespoons butter or margarine
    1 teaspoon poppy seed
    2 tablespoons grated Parmesan
        cheese
    6 brown-and-serve cloverleaf rolls

In foilware pan melt the butter or margarine on the grill. Add poppy seed and grated Parmesan cheese. Separate the sections of cloverleaf rolls and arrange in butter mixture in pan. Brown the pieces of rolls on grill, turning rolls until all sides are toasted.

PORCUPINE MEATBALL—A type of meatball containing rice, which, when cooked, protrudes from the meat in such a way as to resemble the quills of a porcupine. The rice is uncooked when the balls are shaped but swells during cooking in a sauce.

Porcupine Meatballs

    1 slightly beaten egg
    1 10¾-ounce can condensed tomato
        soup
    ¼ cup uncooked long-grain rice
    2 tablespoons finely chopped onion
    1 tablespoon snipped parsley
    ½ teaspoon salt
        Dash pepper
    1 pound ground beef
            • • •
    ½ cup water
    1 teaspoon Worcestershire sauce

Combine beaten egg, ¼ *cup* of the tomato soup, uncooked rice, onion, parsley, salt, and pepper. Add ground beef; mix well. Shape the mixture into 20 meatballs; place in skillet. Mix remaining soup, water, and Worcestershire sauce. Pour over meatballs. Bring to boiling; reduce heat and simmer, covered, for 40 minutes, stirring often. Makes 4 to 5 servings.

PORGY (*pôr′gē*) A lean, saltwater fish that is found in warm, coastal waters throughout the world. One type of porgy, the scup, inhabits the waters along the east coast of North America.

The porgy is a good-eating fish that attains a length of 12 to 18 inches and can weigh up to four pounds. Those sold in markets average two pounds. Fish markets near the coast sell fresh, dressed porgy. They are seldom cut into fillets or shipped inland. Fry, broil, or bake the porgy in a sauce. (See also *Fish.*)

PORK

Leaner breeds of pork produce a wide selection
of tender, meaty cuts for recipe preparation.

When a juicy, tender pork chop is placed before you on the dinner table, you may well say, "That's a nice piece of pork," and you'd be right. But did you know that pork chops come from lean hogs, which make them ideal for low-calorie diets?

Pork is the meat of a hog which is from 4 to 6½ months old, generally weighing 190 to 250 pounds. From this hog you get pork chops, loin cuts, ham, bacon, and a host of other meaty cuts. A pig, on the other hand, is a young animal that hasn't reached market weight—unless for use as a suckling pig. Once the animal weighs 190 pounds, it is called a hog. These hogs are bred and fed to provide lean meat with fewer calories. The too-fat pig of yesteryear is an animal of the past.

Hogs of former years were often large, corpulent beasts that were fattened up to give the appearance of health. As such, they were used by the ancient Egyptians as a sacrifice to the gods, and in later years, by other people as animals possessing magical powers. In those superstitious eras, many farmers planted pig tails or ribs to aid the growth of their crops.

These portly animals have also served as the centerpiece for many medieval feasts; the large untamed hog (or wild boar) with an apple in its mouth and surrounded by potatoes and vegetables was placed on a platter and set on the table. Lacking the social graces of today's pork eater, medieval people would yank off large sections of the meat and eat them out of hand.

Elegant way to prepare a loin roast

← Top Rio Grande Pork Roast with crushed corn chips. Accompany with Bean and Avocado Boats (see *Salad* for recipe).

Not only has the animal changed over the years—in size, leanness, and domesticity—but cooking methods have become sophisticated as is evident in this recipe:

Roast Pork Loin

> 1 3- to 4-pound boneless rolled
>   pork loin roast
> 1 12-ounce jar pineapple preserves
> ⅓ cup horseradish mustard

Place pork on rack in shallow roasting pan. Roast, uncovered, at 325° till meat thermometer registers 170°, about 2½ to 3 hours. Heat preserves and mustard. Brush small amount on meat last 15 minutes of roasting. Pass remaining sauce. Makes 3 to 4 servings per pound.

The large porker was, and still is used for entertainment. Shakespeare referred to greased pig contests where a whole village would try to catch a greased pig. Whoever caught it took it home—hence, the term "bringing home the bacon." Even today, this animal is used at county fairs in greased pig or hog calling contests.

While De Soto was the first to introduce pigs to America (he brought them from Cuba in 1539), the early colonists also included pigs on their ships as they traveled to the New World. Since this animal was well suited to the wild terrain in America, people took the hog along with them as they went westward. Thus, it became one of America's first farm animals.

By the mid-1800s, hog production was important to the economy of the Midwest. So much so, in fact, that canals were built primarily for transporting these animals to the packing plants. Frequently, this was to Cincinnati. In the 1850s, Cincinnati packed or "salted down" so much pork that it became known as "Porkopolis." Fortunately, with the development of the refrigerated railroad car, fresh pork was shipped across the country for all to enjoy so that today, you don't have to live by one of these waterways to enjoy it.

Nutritional value: With the new lean breeds of hogs and the closer trimming of the meat by packers, the fat content of pork is often low, depending on the cut of pork. Consequently, meat from these leaner hogs is good for weight-control diets. A 3½-ounce serving of roasted tenderloin has 240 calories, meat from six roasted, medium-sized spareribs has 246 calories, and one 6-ounce (uncooked weight) loin chop, cooked, has 314 calories. One 2½x2x2½-inch slice of roasted picnic shoulder has about 116 calories, and one 3x2x½-inch slice of roasted Boston shoulder (butt) has 164 calories.

Pork is also noted for its vitamin B content—thiamine, riboflavin, and niacin. In fact, pork has more thiamine than any other single food source. As you know, thiamine is an essential part of the diet for normal functioning of the nervous system, and it helps prevent beriberi.

As with other meats, pork also contains high-quality protein. The meat is 96 to 98 percent digestible, so it should be included in the diet often. Pork also contains minerals such as iron, potassium, phosphorus, and magnesium.

Forms of Pork

It's not only humorous, but true, to say that one can eat just about all of the pig except the squeal. Pork is available in many different cuts as fresh, cured, and cured and smoked. Familiarizing yourself with the portions of the hog from which the different cuts come will help you in identifying the common cuts.

Starting at the front of the animal, shoulder cuts include the Boston shoulder (sometimes referred to as butt) and blade steaks; the picnics and arm cuts are from the upper part of the front legs. The loin area on the top side of the midsection includes the blade loin, rib, center loin, and sirloin cuts. The expression "eating high off the hog" refers to this area, and it probably originated some years ago to signify that when a person changed from his diet of salt pork to eating the meaty loin parts, he was thought to be well-off.

The lower portion, the breast of the hog, produces spareribs and bacon, and the hind legs yield cured and smoked hams and pork leg roasts, also called fresh hams. Even the hocks and feet can be cooked.

Fresh pork: At the packing plant, the carcasses are dressed, chilled, then cut and trimmed into the various market cuts. Trimmed-off fat is used to make lard and other shortenings. Some of the fresh pork cuts are chopped, seasoned, and stuffed into casings for fresh sausage (see also *Sausage*), while some cuts are ground for use in patties and meat loaves.

Occasionally, shoulder cuts are marketed as porklets. This boneless cut has been processed through a machine that scores the surface, breaking muscle fibers.

Even the hog's ears and tail, cooked crisp or used in a sauce, are favorites in some households. Other fresh pork products include liver, heart, chitterlings, pig's feet, and tongue.

Although the majority of pork is sold in cuts, with roasts and chops being the most popular, you can special-order a whole suckling pig (a very young pig that is still nursing, weighing 10 to 12 pounds dressed) or a larger, whole dressed pig.

Cured, and cured and smoked pork: Because of the popular flavor that curing and smoking impart, a large portion of the pork available today is processed in this manner. First, the meat is cured with brine. A limited amount of pork, including some picnics and hams, is cured but not smoked. These cured cuts are often referred to as pickled. Pickled pig's feet have a slightly different pickling cure and are also marketed without being smoked. The majority of the cured cuts, however, are smoked as well as cured. Some of these need additional cooking, such as bacon, while others are ready to eat, as is the case with fully cooked and canned hams. (See *Bacon, Ham* for additional information.)

Tenderloin (left) is the small, tapering, round muscle that lies on one side of the T-bone, about one-third the length of the loin. Since this is a boneless, very tender and lean cut, it can be roasted or braised. Slices from the tenderloin can be panfried. *Sirloin Roast* (upper right) comes from the loin section and contains the hip bone. The largest muscle in this cut is referred to as the loin eye, while the smaller muscle is called the tenderloin and becomes larger as it approaches the hip. Roast this cut. *Loin Chop* (lower right) contains a T-bone and is cut from the center of the loin. The T-bone separates the larger loin eye muscle from the smaller tenderloin muscle. Braise, broil, or panfry this cut of pork.

Fresh Boston Shoulder Roast (top) is occasionally referred to as Boston Butt. It contains a part of the blade bone and comes from the shoulder area of the animal. Roast this cut. *Smoked Shoulder Roll* (or *Butt*) (left) comes from the largest muscle of the Fresh Boston Shoulder Roast. This boneless cut is cured, smoked, and rolled. Roast or simmer this cut in liquid. Slices can be panfried or broiled. *Blade Steak* (right) is a fresh pork cut from the Fresh Boston Shoulder Roast. It can be identified by the blade bone. Braise, broil, or panfry the steaks.

Crown Roast (upper left) is made from the rib sections of two pork loins with six to ten center ribs in each. The ends of the ribs are "frenched" (meat is removed, leaving about 1 inch of each bone exposed) and the backbone is removed. Then, the two sections of pork (with ribs to the outside) are tied together forming a crown. Roast. Center may be filled. *Center Loin Roast* (upper right) is cut from the middle section of the loin. The larger muscle is the loin eye, and the smaller muscle is the tenderloin. The T-bone separates the two muscles and is used for identification. Roast. *Rib Chops* (bottom) are identified by the rib bone. Chops are cut from the rib section of the loin. Muscle present is the loin eye. Extra-thick or two-rib chops are used for stuffed pork chops. Have pockets cut parallel to rib and on rib side of chop. Roast or braise.

Canadian-Style Bacon (left) is made from the boneless loin eye. This formed cut is cured and smoked and is usually available fully cooked. Canadian-style bacon is long and usually round with the characteristic pinkish color of cured and smoked pork. Roast the whole piece or slice and broil, panbroil, or panfry. *Boneless Center Loin Roast* (upper right) is the loin eye, the largest muscle in the loin section, and is cut from the Center Loin Roast. Roast this cut. *Butterfly Chop* (lower right) is made from a boned, thick chop or a boneless loin piece. A slice is made through the fat surface almost all the way through the meat, then it is spread flat, making a butterfly-shaped chop, which appears larger and cooks in less time. Braise or broil this cut of pork.

Back Ribs (left) are also called Country-Style Back Ribs. These meaty ribs contain the rib bones cut from the rib area of the loin. The thicker layer of meat covering the ribs comes from the loin eye muscle. Roast or braise these ribs. *Blade Loin Roast* (upper right) comes from the rib section of the loin next to the shoulder. This roast contains the rib bones on one side and the blade bones at one end. The loin eye is the predominant muscle. Roast this cut. *Rib Chop* (lower right) is identified by the rib bone. It is cut from the rib section of the loin; consequently, it has no tenderloin muscle. The loin eye is the only muscle. Braise, broil, or panfry rib chops.

Spareribs (left) come from the side of pork and contain the breastbone, rib bones, and rib cartilage. Roast, braise, or cook the spareribs in liquid. *Salt Side* (top right), also available as fresh, comes from the side of pork. This cut is characterized by layers of fat and lean and by a salt deposit on the outer surface because of its dry salt cure. It is used primarily for seasoning and can be cooked in liquid, panbroiled, or panfried. *Bacon* (bottom right) is available in a slab, or sliced thin or thick. Bacon comes from the cured and smoked side of pork. Broil, panbroil, or panfry slices. Bacon Squares (not shown) are cured and smoked pieces of pork from the jowl.

Smoked Picnic Shoulders (halves at bottom) are sometimes called callie hams or incorrectly referred to as picnic hams because of their resemblance in flavor to ham. The picnic is cut from the lower shoulder and arm section of the front legs, while a ham is a cured and smoked cut from the hind legs. The picnic contains the shank, arm, and blade bones. The shoulder muscles are interspersed with fat, and skin covers the shank end. Picnics are cured and smoked and can be purchased fully cooked or cook-before-eating. The smoked shoulders are available either as whole or half pieces of the shoulder. A Fresh Picnic Shoulder is the same cut, except that it has not been cured or smoked. Roast or cook these cuts in liquid. *Canned Smoked Picnic Shoulder* (top) is a boneless cut that is fully cooked. These canned picnics come in square or pear-shaped cans and generally weigh three to five pounds. Heat meat or serve it cold.

Smoked Center Loin Roast (center) is cut from the middle section of the loin. It contains the larger loin eye muscle and the smaller tenderloin muscle, and it can be identified by the T-bone. It is the same cut as the fresh cut, except that it is cured and smoked. Generally, this roast is fully cooked and needs only to be heated before serving. *Smoked Loin Chops* are cut from the Smoked Center Loin Roast and also contain the T-bone. The smaller bone separates the loin eye muscle from the tenderloin. Broil or panfry these smoked chops.

Smoked Spareribs (lower left) come from the side of pork and are similar to fresh spareribs, except that smoked ribs are first cured, then smoked. They contain the breastbone, rib bones, and rib cartilage with a thin covering of meat over the ribs. Roast, braise, or cook the smoked spareribs in liquid. *Smoked Hocks* (upper right) are cut from just above the pig's feet. They are then cured and smoked. This bony, shank cut can be identified by the round bone. Fresh hocks are also available and are similar to the smoked hocks, except that the fresh ones are not cured or smoked. To cook fresh or smoked hocks, braise or cook them in liquid.

How to select

Today, with modern breeding techniques, hogs are marketed regularly, making pork available year-round. When selecting from the abundant supply of pork available in the meat counter, there are some hints to keep in mind to ensure that you are buying the quality you expect to get.

Although federal grades have been set up for pork, they are not widely used. Some packers, however, particularly those that pack smoked pork products, often indicate the quality of pork on their packaging by means of different brand names. Even though pork is not usually federally graded, all of the meat that is sold to homemakers has been inspected.

How much pork to buy

Because of the varying amounts of fat and bone in the different pork cuts, the following list is a guide to the average number of servings per pound of pork as purchased. Be sure to allow for hearty appetites.

Cut	Servings per pound
Fresh roast—bone-in sirloin, blade loin, center loin, Boston shoulder, picnic shoulder, leg (fresh ham)	2 to 3
Fresh roast—without bone tenderloin, center loin, rolled shoulder, rolled leg (fresh ham)	3 to 4
Smoked roast—bone-in picnic shoulder, center loin, ham—butt and shank	2 to 3
Smoked roast—without bone shoulder roll (butt), picnic shoulder, ham roll	3 to 4
Fully cooked smoked ham—bone-in	3 to 4
Spareribs	1 to 2

When choosing fresh pork cuts, look for fine-grained meat that is marbled with flecks of white, firm fat. There should also be a uniform covering of firm, white fat on the outside surfaces. The lean portion of the pork cut should be firm and have a light, grayish pink color, and the bones should have a slight pink tint.

You will find that the cuts of pork in greatest demand, such as the center ham slice, spareribs, bacon, and loin chops, tend to have the highest price tags, and often they will be the cuts that are the quickest to cook. However, these select cuts make up only about a third of the animal, so there are many additional cuts that are good for stretching the budget, such as the shoulder and picnic cuts and the shank and butt cuts of ham.

In addition to the fresh, cured, cured and smoked, and canned cuts, there are several other pork products including sausages, made solely with pork or in combination with other meats and spices, canned luncheon meats, packaged sliced meats, and combination dishes. With the increased demand and widespread enjoyment of pork today, there is a greater number of specialty canned and frozen products on the market.

Besides the meat products that come from the hog, there are also some other products that should be mentioned. Lard is one of the most important of these. And one should not forget that gelatin and the casings used in sausages come from the hog as do some pharmaceuticals.

How to store

Fresh, cured, cured and smoked, and cooked pork should be promptly stored in the refrigerator to maintain the best possible quality. When longer storage is desired, use your freezer, following the recommended time limits that are listed.

Fresh pork: Prepackaged meat from the supermarket should be stored in the coldest part of the refrigerator in the original wrapping. Use fresh cuts of pork, ground pork, and variety meats within a day or two after purchase, and fresh sausage within one week of purchase.

Freeze fresh pork quickly in tightly wrapped and sealed, conveniently sized packages. Store at 0° or less. Ground pork can be frozen for up to three months, while other fresh pork cuts can be kept for up to six months. Thaw meat in the refrigerator or during cooking. Allow additional time when cooking a frozen roast.

Cured, and cured and smoked pork: Pork products processed in this manner are perishable, but they keep slightly longer than do the fresh cuts. Refrigerate cured, and cured and smoked pork in the original wrapper no longer than one week. Ham slices should be kept only three to four days. Bacon will keep slightly longer.

Canned hams should be refrigerated unless the label reads otherwise. Unopened, the canned hams will keep several months in the refrigerator. However, check the label directions for suggested storage.

Some cured and smoked cuts, such as shoulder rolls, can be frozen for up to 60 days. If necessary, bacon can be frozen up to one month. Canned hams and other canned meats should not be frozen.

Cooked pork: Cool cooked pork and gravies quickly, then cover or wrap and store in the coldest part of the refrigerator. Leave the cooked meat in pieces as large as possible, although the bones may be removed first. Use within a few days.

Pork Roasting Chart			
Cut	Approximate Weight (Pounds)	Internal Temp. on Removal from Oven	Approximate Cooking Time (Total Time)
Roast meat at constant oven temperature of 325°.			
FRESH PORK			
Boston Shoulder Roast	4 to 6	170°	3 to 4 hrs.
Picnic Shoulder	5 to 8	170°	3 to 4 hrs.
Loin, center	3 to 5	170°	2½ to 3 hrs.
Loin, center; rolled (boneless)	3 to 4	170°	2½ to 3 hrs.
Loin, half	5 to 7	170°	3½ to 4¼ hrs.
Loin, blade or sirloin	3 to 4	170°	2¼ to 2¾ hrs.
Leg (fresh ham)	10 to 16	170°	4½ to 6 hrs.
Leg, half (fresh ham)	5 to 7	170°	3½ to 4½ hrs.
CURED AND SMOKED PORK			
Ham (fully cooked)			
half, boneless	4 to 5	135° to 140°	1½ to 2 hrs.
whole, boneless	8 to 10	135° to 140°	2 to 2¼ hrs.
half	5 to 7	135° to 140°	1¾ to 2¼ hrs.
whole	10 to 14	135° to 140°	2½ to 3 hrs.
Ham (cook-before-eating)			
shank or butt	3 to 4	160°	2 to 2¼ hrs.
half	5 to 7	160°	2½ to 3 hrs.
whole	10 to 14	160°	3½ to 4 hrs.
Picnic shoulder	5 to 8	170°	3 to 4½ hrs.
Shoulder roll (boneless)	2 to 3	170°	1 to 2 hrs.
Canadian-Style bacon	2 to 4	160°	1 to 2½ hrs.

How to Prepare

Most pork cuts are tender pieces of meat, and like other types of meat, pork should be cooked at low to moderate temperatures. The type of cookery that is chosen —dry-heat or moist-heat—depends sometimes on the tenderness of the cut, but usually on the dish that is being prepared. Pork cooked using the proper method will be tender, juicy, and full-flavored.

Dry-heat cookery: Use this type of preparation for the tender cuts of pork. Dry-heat cooking methods (without added moisture) include roasting, broiling or grilling, including cooking on the rotisserie, panbroiling, and panfrying. Cuts that can be prepared by dry-heat cookery include shoulder steaks and roasts, loin cuts, cured and smoked hams, and legs (fresh hams), bacon, Canadian-style bacon, ham slices, and smoked pork chops. Although fresh, thick pork chops are tender cuts, they are frequently braised.

The best way to determine the doneness of roast pork is to use a meat thermometer. Insert it midway in the thickest portion, making sure the tip doesn't touch bone or fat. Until the completion of recent research, the recommended internal temperature for all pork roasting cuts was 185° F. Now, with the exception of smoked pork cuts, 170° F. is accepted as the temperature for optimal degree of doneness for juicy pork of top eating quality.

How to Roast a Pig

Plan on 60 to 70 servings from a pig that weighs about 60 pounds, dressed. (The pig would originally weigh 90 to 100 pounds.) Choose a grassless place for roasting. In a pit 12 inches deep and as wide and long as the pig (or at ground level), arrange charcoal the length

Meal in a dish, ready in a jiffy

←Fully cooked chops are the main feature of Smoked Pork Chop and Lima Skillet. The flavor of the chops permeates the sauce.

of the pig in two rows, about 12 to 15 inches apart. Drive notched pipes into ground to hold spit about 16 inches above the coals. Rig up a motor-driven rotisserie or provide manpower to turn the pig during roasting.

Run spit through center cavity of dressed pig; balance and secure well with wires and/or wire mesh. Tie legs together; cover tail and ears with foil. Have drip pan under pig, between the rows of hot charcoal. Tilt pan slightly to accumulate fat during roasting.

Place unstuffed pig on spit; begin roasting and turning. As it roasts, the pig will shrink—have tools handy to tighten wires. Also have a sprinkler filled with water to put out any flare-ups among coals. (Fires are more frequent during first hour or two of roasting.) Do not baste pig during roasting.

If coals are added to maintain a constant red glow, the 60-pound pig should take about 8 hours to roast. Time will vary, depending on the intensity of heat and weight of pig. The best indicator of doneness is a meat thermometer. Place thermometer in center of "ham" portion making sure thermometer is not resting against bone or on spit rod. When thermometer registers 170° to 185°, the pig is ready to carve. Have a large surface available for this process. Chances are the meat will be so thoroughly cooked it will fall off the bones.

Smoked Pork Chop and Lima Skillet

> 2 10-ounce packages frozen lima beans
> 5 or 6 smoked pork loin chops
> 1 teaspoon chicken-flavored gravy base
> 1 tablespoon all-purpose flour
> ½ teaspoon dried basil leaves, crushed
> ¾ cup water

Omitting salt in cooking water, cook lima beans according to package directions; drain. In skillet brown chops over medium heat. Remove chops. Pour off all but about 1 tablespoon drippings. Add gravy base to skillet. Blend in flour and basil. Add water; cook and stir over medium heat till thickened and bubbly. Add lima beans to skillet; stir to coat. Arrange chops over beans. Cover; cook over low heat till heated, about 5 minutes. Serves 5 or 6.

Glazed Sausage Loaf

2 slightly beaten eggs
1 cup soft rye bread crumbs
  (1¼ slices)
⅓ cup milk
2 tablespoons snipped parsley
2 pounds bulk pork sausage
1 12-ounce package frozen rice
  pilaf, thawed

. . .

1 8-ounce jar strained plums
  (baby food)
2 tablespoons sugar
2 tablespoons lemon juice

Combine eggs, rye bread crumbs, milk, and parsley. Add sausage and rice; mix well. Shape into loaf in shallow baking pan. Bake at 350° for 1 hour. Remove from oven. Spoon off fat.

Combine strained plums, sugar, and lemon juice. Heat the mixture till bubbly. Brush plum mixture on loaf. Bake 15 minutes longer. Pass remaining sauce. Makes 8 servings.

Kraut-Pork Pinwheel

1 pound ground fresh pork
½ cup fine dry bread crumbs
1 slightly beaten egg
1 teaspoon salt
½ teaspoon Worcestershire sauce
  Dash pepper

. . .

1 16-ounce can sauerkraut,
  drained
¼ cup chopped onion
5 bacon slices

Combine ground pork, bread crumbs, slightly beaten egg, salt, Worcestershire sauce, and pepper; mix thoroughly. On waxed paper pat ground meat mixture to a 10x7-inch rectangle.

Snip drained sauerkraut. Combine sauerkraut with onion. Spread evenly over meat. Starting at narrow end, roll up jelly-roll fashion; place seam side down in a shallow baking dish. Arrange bacon across top. Bake at 350° for 40 to 45 minutes. Makes 5 or 6 servings.

For a variation of Glazed Sausage Loaf, omit rice from meat mixture. Pat meat into a 12x10-inch rectangle, then spread the rice atop. Roll up as for jelly roll; seal. Bake as directed.

Glazed Ham Slice

    1 1½-inch slice fully cooked
         ham (about 2 pounds)
    ½ cup brown sugar
    2 tablespoons cornstarch
       Dash ground cloves
       Dash salt
  1½ cups cranberry juice cocktail
    ½ cup orange juice
    ½ cup raisins

Slash fat edge of ham at 2-inch intervals. Insert whole cloves in fat, if desired. Place ham in shallow baking dish. Bake at 325° for 30 minutes. Meanwhile, mix brown sugar, cornstarch, cloves, and salt. Add fruit juices and raisins. Cook and stir till mixture thickens and bubbles. Spoon part of the sauce over the ham; bake till glazed, about 20 minutes longer. Pass remaining sauce. Makes 6 servings.

Stuffed Pork Tenderloin

    2 pork tenderloins of equal size
       Salt
       Pepper
    3 tablespoons chopped onion
    ¼ cup butter or margarine
    4 cups dry bread cubes (about
         7 slices, cut in ½-inch cubes)
    1 6-ounce can sliced mushrooms,
         drained
    ½ teaspoon poultry seasoning
    ½ teaspoon ground sage
    ¼ teaspoon salt
    ¼ teaspoon pepper
    2 to 4 tablespoons water *or*
         chicken broth
       Salt
       Pepper
    4 bacon slices

Have tenderloins split open lengthwise but do not cut through; flatten. Season with salt and pepper. Cook onion in butter. Combine with bread cubes, mushrooms, and next 4 ingredients. Toss with enough liquid to moisten. Spread mixture over one tenderloin; lay other tenderloin on top. Season with salt and pepper and top with bacon slices. Place on rack in shallow roasting pan. Roast, uncovered, at 325° for about 1½ hours. Makes 8 servings.

Choose a thick slice of ham for Glazed Ham Slice. The topper blends the flavors of cranberry juice, orange juice, and raisins.

Rio Grande Pork Roast

    1 4- to 5-pound boneless rolled
         pork loin roast
    ½ teaspoon salt
    ½ teaspoon garlic salt
    ½ teaspoon chili powder
        · · ·
    ½ cup apple jelly
    ½ cup catsup
    1 tablespoon vinegar
    ½ teaspoon chili powder
    1 cup crushed corn chips
       Water

Place pork, fat side up, on rack in shallow roasting pan. Combine the salt, garlic salt, and the ½ teaspoon chili powder; rub into roast. Insert meat thermometer. Roast, uncovered, at 325° till meat thermometer registers 165°, about 2½ to 3 hours.

In small saucepan combine jelly, catsup, vinegar, and ½ teaspoon chili powder. Bring to boiling; reduce heat and simmer, uncovered, for 2 minutes. Brush roast with glaze. Sprinkle top with corn chips. Continue roasting till thermometer registers 170°, about 10 to 15 minutes longer. Remove roast from oven. Let stand 10 minutes. Meanwhile, measure pan drippings including any corn chips. Add water to drippings to make 1 cup. Heat to boiling and pass the sauce with the meat. Makes 3 to 4 servings per pound.

Apple-Buttered Pork Loin

  1 **5- to 6-pound pork loin,**
     boned, rolled, and tied
½ **cup apple butter**
  2 **tablespoons peanut butter**
¼ **teaspoon grated orange peel**
  2 **tablespoons orange juice**

Balance roast on spit. Roast over *medium* coals till meat thermometer registers 170°, about 3 hours. Gradually stir apple butter into peanut butter; add orange peel and juice. Brush over entire surface of roast; continue cooking 15 to 20 minutes. Makes 12 to 16 servings.

Ribs with Onion Sauce

  4 **pounds pork spareribs, cut**
     in serving-sized pieces
  2 **cups sliced onion**
  2 **cloves garlic, minced**
  1 **tablespoon salad oil**
½ **cup water**
¼ **cup vinegar**
¼ **cup chili sauce**
  3 **tablespoons brown sugar**
  2 **tablespoons lemon juice**
  2 **tablespoons Worcestershire sauce**
1½ **teaspoons salt**
  1 **teaspoon dry mustard**

Roast ribs, meaty side down, in shallow roasting pan at 450° for 30 minutes. Drain off excess fat. Turn ribs meaty side up. Cook onion and garlic in hot oil till tender; add remaining ingredients. Simmer 10 minutes. Pour sauce over ribs. Reduce oven temperature to 350°; bake ribs till tender, about 1½ hours, basting occasionally with sauce. If sauce gets too thick, add more water. Makes 4 to 6 servings.

Moist-heat cookery: This type of cookery is used for very lean cuts, less-tender cuts, or cuts that would be improved with the addition of moisture. Braising and cooking in liquid are methods of moist-heat cookery. Pork cuts that often are braised include chops, ribs, tenderloins, and shoulder or blade steaks. Cuts cooked in liquid include spareribs, hocks, pig's feet, and smoked shoulder cuts.

Glazed Smoked Shoulder

  1 **2- to 3-pound smoked pork**
     shoulder roll (boneless)
    Water
  1 **medium onion, sliced**
  3 **whole cloves**
  1 **bay leaf**
  1 **3-inch stick cinnamon**
½ **teaspoon celery seed**

      • • •

½ **cup brown sugar**
  1 **tablespoon all-purpose flour**
½ **teaspoon dry mustard**
⅛ **teaspoon ground cloves**
  2 **tablespoons water**

Place pork in large Dutch oven; cover with water. Add onion, whole cloves, bay leaf, cinnamon stick, and celery seed. Cover tightly; simmer 2 hours. Remove meat from liquid. Place meat on rack in shallow roasting pan. Combine remaining ingredients. Brush on meat. Bake at 350° for 20 to 30 minutes. Serves 6 to 8.

Best Barbecued Ribs

Cut 2 pounds pork spareribs or back ribs in 2 large pieces. Simmer the ribs, covered, in enough salted water to cover till tender, about 45 to 60 minutes; drain.

  Meanwhile, prepare sauce: In saucepan combine ¼ cup catsup, 2 tablespoons chili sauce, 1 tablespoon brown sugar, 1 tablespoon butter or margarine, and 1 tablespoon chopped onion. Add 2 teaspoons prepared mustard, 1 teaspoon Worcestershire sauce, dash garlic salt, and 2 thin lemon slices. Bring the mixture to boiling; remove the mixture from heat.

  Grill hot ribs over slow to medium coals about 10 to 15 minutes on each side, brushing often with sauce. (Or place hot ribs in shallow roasting pan; pour sauce over. Bake at 350° about 20 to 25 minutes, basting with sauce occasionally. Makes 2 servings.

Ribs for a barbecue treat

When you can't prepare Best Barbecued →
Ribs outdoors on the grill, put them in a pan, pour sauce over, and bake in oven.

Braised Pork Chops

Brown ¾- to 1-inch thick pork chops slowly on both sides in small amount hot shortening; pour off excess fat. Season; add a little hot water, if desired. Cover tightly; cook over low heat till tender, about 45 to 60 minutes. Make gravy from pan juices, if desired.

Pork Chops in Sour Cream

    6 loin pork chops, ½ inch thick
    ¾ teaspoon dried sage leaves,
       crushed
    ½ teaspoon salt
      Dash pepper
    2 tablespoons shortening
    2 medium onions, sliced
    1 beef bouillon cube
    ¼ cup boiling water
    ½ cup dairy sour cream
    1 tablespoon all-purpose flour
    2 tablespoons snipped parsley

Rub chops with mixture of sage, salt, and pepper. Brown lightly on both sides in hot shortening. Drain off excess fat. Add onions. Dissolve bouillon cube in water. Pour over chops. Cover and simmer till tender, 30 minutes. Remove meat. Combine sour cream and flour in bowl. Slowly stir in meat drippings. Return mixture to skillet; cook and stir just till boiling. Add water till gravy is desired consistency. Serve over chops. Trim with parsley. Serves 6.

Orange-Glazed Pork Chops

    4 pork chops, ¾ inch thick
    1 tablespoon shortening
      Salt and pepper
    ½ cup orange juice
    2 tablespoons brown sugar
    2 tablespoons orange marmalade
    1 tablespoon vinegar

In skillet brown chops on both sides in hot shortening. Season with salt and pepper. Drain off excess fat. Combine orange juice, brown sugar, marmalade, and vinegar; pour over chops. Cover and simmer till chops are tender, about 45 minutes. Remove chops to warm platter. Spoon sauce over the chops. Makes 4 servings.

Cheese-Noodle Casserole

    1 pound diced uncooked pork
    1 tablespoon shortening
    1 10½-ounce can condensed
      chicken-rice soup
    ½ cup chopped green pepper
    ¼ cup chopped canned pimiento
    1 17-ounce can cream-style corn
    8 ounces sharp process American
      cheese, shredded (2 cups)
    4 ounces medium noodles

In skillet brown pork in hot shortening. Stir in soup; cover and simmer till tender, about 45 to 60 minutes. Stir in remaining ingredients *except* noodles. Cook noodles according to package directions; drain. Stir into pork mixture. Turn into a 2-quart casserole. Bake, covered, at 350° for 45 minutes. Makes 6 servings.

How to serve

Carving some of the pork roasts can be a real challenge unless you are familiar with the proper techniques. (For carving ham, crown roast, and blade loin roast, see *Carving*.) To carve the picnic shoulder, remove a slice from the bottom surface (parallel to the large bone) so that the shoulder will sit flat as it is carved. Then, find where the elbow (smaller bone) and arm bone (larger bone) are joined together. Make a cut down to the larger arm bone and cut along this bone. Remove the entire piece of meat. Slice this section. Then, remove the meat on either side of the larger arm bone and slice.

Pork roasts are not the only cuts that make delicious entrées. Other forms of pork can be used in sandwiches, casseroles, salads, and soups. (See also *Meat*.)

Pork Salad Jamboree

A good use for leftover cooked pork roast—

Sprinkle 1 cup cubed, unpeeled apple with 1 tablespoon lemon juice. Toss with 2 cups cubed, cooked pork, 1 cup halved and seeded red grapes, ½ cup chopped celery, ½ cup mayonnaise or salad dressing, and ½ teaspoon salt. Chill thoroughly. Makes 4 or 5 servings.

Hearty Hodgepodge is remindful of an old-fashioned soup, only this version contains garbanzo beans, Polish sausage, and both a ham hock and a beef shank. Pass French bread.

Hearty Hodgepodge

6 slices bacon
1 medium onion, thinly sliced
1 1-pound beef shank
1 ¾ -pound ham hock
6 cups water
2 teaspoons salt
2 15-ounce cans garbanzo beans
3 cups diced, peeled potatoes
1 clove garlic, minced
1 4-ounce link Polish sausage, thinly sliced
Toasted and buttered French bread

In Dutch oven cook bacon till crisp; draining, reserving 2 tablespoons drippings. Crumble bacon and set aside. Add sliced onion to reserved drippings in pan. Cook till tender but not brown. Add beef shank, ham hock, water, and salt. Cover and simmer for 1½ hours.

Remove meat from beef shank and ham hock; dice meat and discard bones. Carefully skim fat from broth. Return diced meat to soup. Add undrained garbanzo beans, potatoes, and garlic. Simmer, covered, 30 minutes longer.

Add sliced Polish sausage and the crumbled bacon. Continue simmering, covered, for 15 minutes. Spoon into soup bowls and serve with toasted French bread. Makes 8 to 10 servings.

Chopped Meat Suey

    1 pound ground pork
    1 chicken bouillon cube
    1 cup boiling water
    2 cups celery, cut in 1-inch
        pieces
    1/3 cup green onions (with tops),
        cut in 1/2-inch pieces
    2 tablespoons cornstarch
    1/3 cup cold water
    1 tablespoon molasses
    1 tablespoon soy sauce
    1 16-ounce can chop suey vegetables,
        drained
      Hot cooked rice

In skillet brown pork; spoon off excess fat. Dissolve bouillon cube in boiling water; add to meat. Stir in celery and onions. Cook, covered, over medium-low heat till vegetables are almost crisp-tender, about 10 minutes.

Mix cornstarch with cold water; add molasses and soy sauce. Stir into meat mixture. Cook and stir till mixture is thickened and bubbly. Add drained vegetables; cook till heated through. Serve over rice. Pass additional soy sauce, if desired. Makes 4 servings.

Sausage and Muffin Bake

    3 English muffins, split and
        toasted
    1/2 pound bulk pork sausage
    1/2 pound ground beef
    1/2 teaspoon salt
    4 ounces sharp process American
        cheese, shredded (1 cup)
          . . .
    1 envelope onion sauce mix
    1 1/2 cups milk
    2 beaten eggs
    1 large tomato, cut in 6 slices

Place an English muffin half in each of 6 buttered 1-cup casseroles. In medium skillet combine meats and salt. Brown meat; drain off excess fat. Divide meat mixture between casseroles; sprinkle with the cheese.

Combine onion sauce mix and milk; stir in eggs. Pour about 1/3 cup egg mixture into each casserole. Top each with a tomato slice. Bake at 350° for 15 to 20 minutes. Serves 6.

Barbecued Pork

    3 tablespoons chopped onion
    1 tablespoon butter or margarine
    1 8-ounce can tomato sauce
    2 tablespoons brown sugar
    1 to 2 teaspoons Worcestershire
        sauce
    1 teaspoon lemon juice
    1 teaspoon prepared mustard
          . . .
    1 cup cubed, cooked pork
    2 hamburger buns, toasted

In saucepan cook onion in butter till tender but not brown. Stir in tomato sauce, brown sugar, Worcestershire sauce, lemon juice, and prepared mustard. Simmer about 20 minutes. Add cooked pork. Heat 10 minutes. Spoon sauce over toasted bun halves. Makes 2 servings.

Minestrone Bake

    1 pound ground pork
    1/2 cup chopped onion
          . . .
    1 10 3/4-ounce can condensed
        minestrone soup
    1 10 1/2-ounce can condensed cream
        of mushroom soup
    1 8-ounce can cut green beans,
        drained
    3 medium raw potatoes, peeled
        and cubed (3 cups)
    1 cup milk

In skillet brown ground pork and chopped onion. Drain off excess fat. Stir in minestrone soup, mushroom soup, drained beans, cubed potatoes, and milk. Turn mixture into 2-quart casserole. Bake, covered, at 350° for 1 hour. Uncover; bake till potatoes are done, about 30 to 45 minutes longer. Makes 6 servings.

PORRIDGE—The British name for cooked oatmeal. Other meal may be substituted for the oatmeal. (See also *Oatmeal*.)

PORRINGER—A small metal bowl with one handle. Originally designed for eating porridge, it is now also used for serving items such as nuts, candies, and sauces.

PORT—A sweet, dessert wine. Port was originally named after Oporto, Portugal, a city at the mouth of the Douro River. The original port was made in the Douro Valley in northern Portugal. However, several other countries, including the United States, produce a similar wine. If the port is not a Portuguese wine, the label must indicate where the port is made. Familiar designations are California Port, New York Port, or American Port.

The early Portuguese port wines were rough and harsh tasting. However, the Portuguese in the Douro Valley experimented with port until they came up with a wine that was much more appealing to their English customers who preferred a sweeter, smoother wine. The wines they developed were mostly sweet-tasting, to which brandy was added during production.

How port is produced: This wine is made from several grape varieties, all of which grow on the steep slopes in northern Portugal. Two types of grapes are important in the making of port: one type, which lacks color and body, gives the wine its character, and the other contributes color. Some of the grape varieties used include the Tintas, Tourigas, and Mouriscos.

The grapes are harvested in late September or early October after which there is usually a festival. The grapes are placed in large troughs where the traditional method is to trample the grapes by foot. However, mechanical crushers have replaced the foot. The juice starts to ferment and is allowed to continue fermenting for a short time until the desired amount of grape sugar remains in the juice. At this point brandy is added, which immediately stops the fermentation process. The juice that remains in the skins is pressed out and made into the brandy that is used to stop fermentation.

Kinds of port: Top-quality port is called vintage port. It is made only in certain years from a select variety of grapes. Most generally, vintage port is bottled at its destination because of the heavy sediment it produces. The longer that vintage port ages in the bottle, the better it becomes and the more costly it is.

Another type of Portuguese port wine, crusted port, is similar to vintage port, except that it is a blend of several vintages rather than from a single vintage. It gets its name from the heavy crust or sediment that forms as the wine is aged for a long period of time.

Wood ports include both the tawny and ruby port and are so named because they are aged in wooden casks. Ruby is aged in wooden casks about three to four years; tawny, about five to six years. Tawny port changes color from the original purple to red with a brown tinge, while ruby port retains its dark red color. The additional aging of the wine causes the color change of tawny port.

White port from Portugal is produced from white grapes, using the same techniques as are used to make the red wines.

Most of the port consumed in the United States is produced either in this country, primarily in California and New York, or imported from Portugal. The imported Portuguese wines are usually those that have been aged in wooden casks.

Although some of the Tinta grapes, which are used in Portuguese wines, have been planted in California, the majority of the American ports are made from grapes other than those used in the ports made in Portugal. Look for the word Tinta on the label of a California port for a wine that most resembles the Portuguese type. Like some Portuguese wines, many American ports are also aged in wood before bottling.

How to use: Port served with cheese and nuts is delightful at the end of a meal. Remember, however, that because the vintage, crusted, and aged ports have a sediment, they should be carefully decanted so that the sediment remains in the bottle. Serve port at a cool room temperature in a regular 8- to 10-ounce wineglass, filling it only part way so that the delightful bouquet of the wine, entrapped in the glass, can be enjoyed. Or serve port in a 5-ounce dessert wineglass.

In addition to being enjoyed as a beverage, port is also used in the preparation of some cheeses, sauces, fruit cups and compotes, jellies, desserts, and salads. (See also *Wines and Spirits.*)

Cranberry-Wine Salad

    2 3-ounce packages raspberry-
        flavored gelatin
    2 cups boiling water
    1 16-ounce can whole cranberry
        sauce
    1 8¾-ounce can crushed pineapple,
        undrained
    ¾ cup port
    ¼ cup chopped walnuts

Dissolve gelatin in boiling water. Stir in the cranberry sauce, *undrained* pineapple, and port. Chill till partially set. Fold in the nuts. Pour gelatin mixture into a 6½-cup mold. Chill till firm. Makes 10 to 12 servings.

Hot Fruit Medley

A dessert specialty made in a chafing dish—

    1 13½-ounce can pineapple chunks
    1 16-ounce can apricot halves
    1 16-ounce can peach halves
    1 16-ounce can pitted dark sweet
        cherries
    ¼ cup brown sugar
    ¼ teaspoon ground cinnamon
    ⅓ cup port
    1 tablespoon lemon juice

Drain pineapple and apricots, reserving *all* of pineapple syrup and ½ *cup* of apricot syrup. Drain other fruits well; set aside. In blazer pan of chafing dish, blend together sugar and cinnamon; add reserved syrups, port, and lemon juice. Heat over direct heat till bubbly. Add pineapple, apricots, and peaches; heat through. Add cherries. Makes 8 servings.

Port du Salut is great for desserts or appetizers.

PORT DU SALUT CHEESE (*port' duh suh loo'*)—A semisoft, ripened, creamy, mild- to strong-flavored cheese made from cow's milk. It is also referred to as Port Salut.

Originally, it was made at the abbey of the Trappist monks in Port du Salut, France, after which this cheese is named. However, it is now also made in other parts of Europe, in Canada, and in the United States. (See also *Cheese*.)

PORTER—A dark, heavy beer that contains browned malt. (See also *Beer*.)

PORTERHOUSE STEAK—A tender beef steak that is cut from the center loin. It is the largest of the steaks having a T-shaped bone and is easily identified by its large tenderloin muscle. (See also *Beef*.)

Swank Porterhouse Steak

    ½ cup finely chopped onion
    1 tablespoon butter or margarine
    1 clove garlic, minced
      Dash salt
      Dash pepper
      Dash celery salt
    1 2½- to 3-pound Porterhouse
        steak, cut 2 inches thick
    ¼ cup dry red wine
    2 tablespoons soy sauce
    ½ teaspoon cornstarch
    1 tablespoon cold water
    2 tablespoons butter, melted
    1 3-ounce can sliced mushrooms,
        drained

In small saucepan cook onion in 1 tablespoon butter till tender. Combine with garlic, salt, pepper, and celery salt. Slash fat along edges of steak. Slitting from fat side, cut pocket in each side of lean meat, almost to bone. Fill pockets with onion mixture. Combine wine and soy sauce; brush some on steak. Grill over *hot* coals or broil till desired doneness, about 25 to 30 minutes for medium-rare. Turn once. Brush occasionally with soy mixture. Blend cornstarch with the cold water. Combine with remaining soy mixture (about 3 tablespoons), 2 tablespoons butter, and mushrooms. Heat and stir till bubbly. Serve with steak. Slice meat across grain. Makes 4 servings.

PORTUGUESE COOKERY—A type of cooking done in Portugal that blends a variety of ingredients into tasty and appealing foods and individual dishes.

Foods commonly used in Portuguese recipes, many of which are flavored with herbs and spices, include olive oil, garlic, figs, eggs, seafood, rice, and nuts (almonds and walnuts). The variety of dishes and flavorings that make up this cuisine are partially attributed to the famous explorers who set out from Portugal and brought back their finds from far-off lands. For example, curry, used primarily as a flavoring in peasant cooking, is one of the spices brought from India by Vasco da Gama in the late fifteenth century.

Portugal has some dishes that are considered to be national favorites. Soups include a chicken broth called *canja* and dry bread soups called *açorda*, which are made with soaked bread and garlic. Vegetables, meat, poultry, or seafood is added,

depending on what is available. The soup is often seasoned with fresh coriander and topped with a raw egg that cooks as it is stirred into the hot mixture.

Because of Portugal's seaboard location, main dishes often consist of fish and shellfish. A seafood stew called *caldeirada* is a mingling of both freshwater and saltwater varieties flavored with cumin and parsley. Although cod is not caught in the waters bordering Portugal, it is considered the national fish. Each year Portuguese fishermen travel to Newfoundland to fish for cod. The catch, which is salt-cured and dried, is used extensively throughout the country. While the preparation of cod varies, a popular method of serving the cooked salt fish is in codfish cakes, which are topped with poached eggs.

A wide variety of meats are eaten in Portugal, including poultry and game. Some people enjoy tripe, which is often prepared with beans. Occasionally, the

Choose a thick cut of meat for preparing Swank Porterhouse Steak. Fill pockets in steak with a seasoned onion-garlic mixture. Then, brush with a sauce of wine and soy as it cooks.

meats are cooked with wine, or the cooked meat is drizzled with lemon juice.

Desserts sometimes consist of cheese, fruit, and nuts, or perhaps a caramel custard, called *pudim flan*, another national dish. Many of the sweets served for dessert are rich with eggs and are often accompanied by port or coffee.

Nogados (Portuguese Christmas Log)

Deep-fat fried pastry strips with a honey glaze—

     1¼ cups sifted all-purpose flour
      1 tablespoon sugar
      ¼ teaspoon salt
      2 tablespoons shortening
      2 beaten eggs
      ½ teaspoon grated lemon peel
      ½ cup sugar
      ½ cup honey
      ½ teaspoon vanilla

In large bowl sift together flour, the 1 tablespoon sugar, and the salt. Cut in shortening till mixture resembles coarse crumbs. Add eggs and lemon peel; mix well. Turn out onto lightly floured surface. Roll dough to 15x12-inch rectangle, ⅛ inch thick. Cut crosswise into five 3-inch wide pieces; cut each piece into strips ¼ inch wide and 3 inches long. Fry a few at a time in deep, hot fat (375°) for about 4 minutes, turning once or twice. Remove with a slotted spoon and drain on paper toweling.

When all the strips have been fried, prepare glaze: Combine the ½ cup sugar and the honey in a small saucepan. Cook and stir till mixture is boiling; continue cooking to hard-ball stage (255°). Stir in vanilla. On well-greased baking sheet, drizzle half the honey-sugar glaze over strips, tossing them to coat all sides. With moistened hands, shape strips quickly into a round log, about 10 inches long and 3 inches wide. Drizzle remaining glaze over top and sides of log. Slice the log thinly to serve.

A trio of Portuguese sweets

← Prepare a Portuguese-inspired dessert—nut-topped Rabanados, sugar-coated Dreams, or Portuguese Christmas Log.

Rabanados

Ladyfingers laced with wine syrup and nuts—

      1 3-ounce package ladyfingers
          (7), split
      2 well-beaten eggs
              • • •
      ½ cup sugar
      ½ cup water
        Dash ground cinnamon
      1 tablespoon port
        Pine nuts

Dip ladyfinger halves into beaten eggs, coating each completely. Fry ladyfingers in deep, hot fat (375°), about 2 minutes on each side, turning once. Drain on paper toweling.

Place ladyfingers in ovenproof serving dish; keep warm in oven. To make syrup, in a saucepan combine sugar, water, and cinnamon. Bring to boiling; boil till slightly thickened, about 10 minutes. Stir in wine. Simmer 3 to 4 minutes more. Pour some of the hot syrup over ladyfingers in dish. Sprinkle with additional ground cinnamon and a few pine nuts. Pass remaining syrup. Makes 8 to 10 servings.

Sonhos (Dreams)

      ½ cup water
      ¼ cup butter or margarine
      2 teaspoons sugar
        Dash salt
      ½ cup sifted all-purpose flour
      2 eggs
      ½ cup sugar
      1 teaspoon ground cinnamon

In saucepan combine water, butter or margarine, the 2 teaspoons sugar, and the salt. Bring to boiling, stirring till butter melts. Add flour all at once. Cook and stir over low heat till mixture forms a ball that does not separate. Remove from heat and vigorously beat in eggs, one at a time, till mixture is smooth and shiny. Drop by rounded teaspoonfuls into deep, hot fat (375°); fry till golden brown, about 4 minutes, turning once. Remove with slotted spoon and drain on paper toweling.

Combine the ½ cup sugar and the cinnamon. Shake puffs in sugar mixture till thoroughly coated. Makes about 2½ dozen.

POSSET (*pos' it*)—A beverage that is made by curdling milk with ale or wine. It is often sweetened and spiced.

POTAGE (*pô tazh'*)—The French word for soup. A good example, Potage Saint Germain, a dish that often appears on restaurant menus, is made with fresh peas.

POTATO—An edible, white tuber used as a vegetable. The word potato has been adapted from the Spanish word *potata*. The hard, white interior of a raw potato is encased by a skin that is off-white, brown, or red in color and paper-thin or moderately thick. Although white potatoes seem similar to sweet potatoes and yams in appearance and use, they are not related.

Now one of the world's most important foods, potatoes first grew in the Andes Mountains of Peru and Chile. Dried potatoes and potato motifs found in second-century South American remains indicate that Indian tribes of that time used potatoes for food. However, not until Spanish explorers arrived in that area 14 centuries later were people from other continents introduced to potatoes.

Before long, the people of many countries were eating this staple food. The Spanish introduced potatoes into Europe, and shortly thereafter potatoes were a dietary staple throughout Europe, Asia, and North America. The Irish quickly incorporated potatoes into their diets. In fact, they became so dependent on this vegetable that the potato famine of 1846 forced thousands of them to flee to Europe and the United States. A French scientist, Antoine-Auguste Parmentier, promoted the use of potatoes in his country in the 1770s as did Frederick the Great of Prussia (now Germany). The influx of potatoes into China began during the seventeenth century. A group of Irishmen in New Hampshire in 1719 are credited with establishing potatoes as a major crop in the United States.

At the same time that potato use was expanding, folklore linked with potato cultivation (some of which is still followed today) had its beginnings. For example, according to superstition, a potato crop should be planted at night during a new moon so that the plants will thrive. If planted on Good Friday, however, the resulting crop will supposedly be poor. And once pulled from the ground, potato storage stability is thought to be ensured only if the entire family eats the first ones harvested.

Potatoes have played various roles in the treatment of certain disorders, too. Many people have carried them in their pockets as a means of warding off rheumatism and sciatica. But in Holland, it is believed that only a stolen potato brings about such a cure. In the United States, potatoes have been used for the cure and prevention of warts and for the treatment of black eyes. Newfoundlanders have tied sliced baked potatoes around their necks to alleviate sore throats, and the Irish have rubbed boiled potato water on aches, sprains, and broken bones.

How potatoes are produced: The major United States commercial production of potatoes is carried on in Idaho, Maine, California, and New York, although many other states produce potatoes on a smaller scale. Growing conditions are controlled as closely as is humanly possible.

For optimum tuber formation, potato plants require a certain number of daylight hours, sufficient moisture to prevent the plants from drying out but not too much moisture to cause rotting (irrigation is sometimes necessary), rich silty soil, and temperatures from 50° to 60°.

Propagation involves planting the "eyes" or cut-up tubers of potatoes rather than seeds. At maturity, the tubers are mechanically dug out of the ground.

The largest percentage of the potato crop is harvested between September and November, but storage facilities enable potatoes to be marketed year-round. Cool but not refrigerated air is recirculated in storage rooms located on the individual farms or at grower association centers.

Potatoes a' plenty

Although white potatoes (center), sweet → potatoes (left), and yams (rear) have similar uses, they are not related.

Nutritional value: Potatoes have been unnecessarily maligned as starchy vegetables that are high in calories. As with so many other foods, however, it's the other foods added, such as the butter, sour cream, sauce, or cooking fat, that give the bulk of calories. In fact, one potato 2½ inches in diameter yields only 76 calories.

This same portion of potato also makes a valuable contribution of Vitamin C and the B vitamin niacin, and a fair contribution of the B vitamin thiamine. Since the major portion of the vitamins and minerals is in or just beneath the skin, eating the skin of baked potatoes provides the diner with a bonus of nutrients.

Types of potatoes: There are many varieties of potatoes. Each is developed for one of three reasons: it will grow under specific conditions, it can be used for a specific cooking purpose, or it will mature at a predetermined time. In general, the varieties range in shape from oblong to round and in skin color from creamy white to red and russet brown. Government regulations permit application of a harmless red dye or wax to red potatoes, but this addition must be labeled on the package. Some widely marketed varieties are Russet Burbank, Red Pontiac, White Rose, Cherokee, Irish Cobbler, and "new" potatoes.

Russet Burbanks, the most well-known variety, are frequently called Idaho potatoes because they are so widely produced in that state. They are oval in shape and have heavily netted, rough brown (russeted) skins and white interiors. They are best used for baking or French-frying.

Red Pontiacs may be round to oblong. Their intense red skins are smooth. The white flesh is very good when boiled.

White Roses are large and elliptical in shape. They have smooth, yellow white skins and a white flesh that makes them especially suitable for boiling.

Cherokees have a round to elliptical shape that is quite often flattened toward the stem end. These potatoes are used for both boiling and baking.

Irish Cobblers are round with white, smooth skins. They are used for boiling.

"New" potatoes are not a specific potato variety. They may be one of several varieties that are harvested while still immature. Their sizes and shapes are determined by the variety of the potato. The thin, delicate skins often appear to have been feathered (an effect 'of mechanical harvesting). New potatoes are used primarily for boiling.

How to select: Although the development of potato varieties that possess all-purpose cooking characteristics is a recent trend, many still are best used for a specific cooking purpose. In general, round-shaped potatoes have firm, waxy interiors that are best suited for boiling. The interiors of long, oval potatoes are characterized as being mealy and make the best baked, fried, or mashed products.

Look for fresh potatoes that are sound and smooth, that have shallow eyes, and that are free of blemishes. There should be no large cuts or bruises. Avoid those with patches of green on the skin, as they have been subjected to light and are bitter and inedible. Do not choose potatoes that are sprouting or appear shriveled. Select uniform-sized potatoes so that all will cook in about the same time.

In addition to fresh potatoes, there are an increasing number of convenience forms that eliminate cooking steps.

How to store: Store all potatoes in a cool (about 55°), dark place. Under these conditions, mature varieties will keep several months. New potatoes do not keep well and should be stored for only a few days.

Potatoes are very sensitive to other storage temperatures. If the storage area is too cold (29° or less), the potatoes will freeze. Even 35° to 40° temperatures cause the starch in the potatoes to convert to sugar more quickly. This results in a dark, fried product and gives the potatoes an astringent flavor.

How to prepare: Prior to cooking, scrub the potato surfaces thoroughly with a vegetable brush. Remove any sprouts or green areas. Personal preference and ultimate use largely determine whether the potatoes are cooked with skins on or off.

The skins can be left on for baking or boiling. To bake potatoes, select uniform-sized baking varieties. After scrubbing, rub the skins with shortening if a soft skin is desired. Prick the potatoes with a fork to allow steam that forms during baking to escape. Bake at 425° for 40 to 60 minutes. If the potatoes are cooked with other foods, bake at 350° to 375° for 70 to 80 minutes. When done, roll the potatoes gently with the palm of your hand to make them mealy. Cut crisscrosses in the tops with a fork. Press the ends to push up the centers slightly, then top with butter or other topping. To foil bake, scrub, prick, and wrap in foil. Bake at 350° for 1½ hours.

Baked Potato Toppers

Whip 1 cup shredded sharp process cheese and ¼ cup soft butter till these ingredients are fluffy. Add ½ cup dairy sour cream and 2 tablespoons snipped green onion; whip.

Soften one 8-ounce package cream cheese. Add ⅓ cup light cream; beat till fluffy. Add 1 tablespoon snipped chives, 1½ teaspoons lemon juice, and ½ teaspoon garlic salt; blend the ingredients together well.

Whole potatoes boiled in skins should be cooked, covered, in boiling, salted water. The potatoes may be scored around the center prior to cooking to facilitate skin removal later. Cooking time varies from 25 to 40 minutes, depending on the potato size. The smaller new potatoes require only 15 to 20 minutes of cooking.

To prepare potatoes for cooking with the skins off, immerse the peeled potatoes or potato pieces in cold water until all the potatoes have been prepared. This prevents the cut surfaces from darkening.

Peeled potatoes may be boiled whole, quartered, or cubed, depending on the final use. Cook the potato pieces, tightly covered, in a small amount of boiling, salted water. Cooking time varies with the piece size: whole potatoes require from 25 to 40 minutes; quarters, from 20 to 25 minutes; and cubes, from 10 to 15 minutes.

Peeled raw potatoes may also be prepared for roasting or frying. Roasted potatoes must be parboiled to speed cooking time. Fried potatoes, raw or precooked, may be pan- or deep-fat fried.

Oven-Browned Potatoes

Peel medium potatoes; cook in boiling, salted water for 15 minutes. Drain. About 45 minutes before meat roast is done (oven temperature 325°), place hot potatoes in drippings around roast, turning potatoes to coat. Roast till done.

How to use: It's hard to beat the versatility of potatoes. Their mild flavor combines well with so many other seasonings and foods that it is possible to serve them several times a day without monotony. Popular herbs and spices that are often used in combination with potatoes include basil leaf, bay leaf, caraway seed, celery seed, dill, mace, marjoram, mustard, nutmeg, oregano, poppy seed, rosemary, savory, cinnamon, sage, and thyme.

As a vegetable side dish, potatoes taste good by themselves, in combination with other vegetables, or in seasoned sauces. Baked potatoes and French fries are probably the most popular serving versions, but other well-known and well-liked concoctions include mashed potatoes, creamed potatoes, hashbrowns, cottage-fries, twice-baked potatoes, duchess potatoes, and scalloped potatoes.

Hashed Browns

Boil 3 medium potatoes in jackets; chill. Peel and shred to make 3 cups. Add 1 to 2 tablespoons grated onion, 1 teaspoon salt, and dash pepper. Melt ¼ cup butter or margarine in 10-inch skillet. Pat potatoes into pan, leaving ½-inch space around edge. Brown about 9 minutes. Reduce heat, if necessary. Cut with spatula to make 4 wedges; turn. Brown till golden, about 7 minutes longer. Makes 4 servings.

Mashed Potatoes

Peel potatoes. Cook in boiling, salted water till tender. Drain; shake over low heat to dry. Remove pan from heat. Mash with potato masher or electric mixer, using lowest speed. Gradually add hot milk as needed and continue beating till light and fluffy. Add salt, pepper, and butter or margarine, as desired.

Crisscross Potatoes

Scrub 3 medium baking potatoes; halve the potatoes lengthwise. Make diagonal slashes, about 1/8 inch deep, in cut surfaces of potatoes, forming a crisscross pattern. Brush the cut surfaces with 2 tablespoons melted butter; season the potatoes with salt and pepper. Arrange them in a baking dish. Bake at 350° for 1 hour. Sprinkle potatoes with paprika; continue baking 15 minutes more. Makes 6 servings.

Scalloped Potato Bake

      8 cups thinly sliced, peeled
          potatoes
   1/4 cup finely chopped onion
      1 10 1/2-ounce can condensed
          cream of mushroom soup
      1 10 1/2-ounce can condensed
          cream of celery soup
      1 cup milk
   3/4 teaspoon salt

Spread *4 cups* sliced potatoes in bottom of a greased 11 3/4x7 1/2x1 3/4-inch baking dish. Combine the next 5 ingredients and dash pepper; pour *half* of the mixture over the potatoes. Repeat layers. Cover; bake in a 350° oven for approximately 1 hour. Uncover and bake 30 to 45 minutes longer. Makes 8 servings.

Score raw potato around center, then boil. Hold potato with a fork speared into the scored area and peel from center out.

Blue Cheese-Bacon Potatoes

      4 medium baking potatoes
   1/2 cup dairy sour cream
      1 ounce blue cheese, crumbled
          (1/4 cup)
   1/4 cup milk
   1/4 cup butter or margarine
   3/4 teaspoon salt
          Dash pepper
      4 slices bacon, crisp-cooked,
          drained, and crumbled

Scrub potatoes; rub with shortening. Bake at 400° till potatoes are done, about 1 hour. Remove from oven; cut a lengthwise slice from top of each potato. Scoop out inside of each; mash. Add sour cream, blue cheese, milk, butter or margarine, salt, and pepper to mashed potatoes; beat with electric mixer till fluffy.

Spoon mixture lightly into potato shells. Place on baking sheet; return to oven till heated through, about 15 minutes. Sprinkle each with crumbled bacon. Makes 4 servings.

Quick Dill Potatoes

Add 2 1/2 cups cubed, peeled potatoes, 2 tablespoons finely chopped onion, and 1 teaspoon salt to 1/3 cup boiling water. Cover and cook for about 15 minutes. Add 1/2 cup light cream; simmer the mixture for about 5 minutes, stirring occasionally. Sprinkle with dried dillweed and pepper. Makes 4 servings.

Potatoes in Lemon Sauce

      2 pounds potatoes
   1/4 cup butter or margarine
      1 tablespoon lemon juice
      1 tablespoon snipped green
          onion tops
          Dash pepper
          Dash ground nutmeg
      1 teaspoon grated lemon peel

Peel potatoes; cook, covered, in boiling, salted water till done, about 30 minutes. Drain and set aside. In small saucepan heat butter with next 4 ingredients. Pour over potatoes, coating each potato well. Sprinkle with grated lemon peel. Makes 6 servings.

As an ingredient in recipes, potatoes can be the background or major flavor of soups, stews, breads, casseroles, and salads. Favorite potato soups come in hot and cold versions. Steaming hot potato soup can serve either as an appetite booster at a first course or as the substantial main dish accompanied by a sandwich. Feature the famous cold soup, vichyssoise, at your next dinner for special guests.

Potato Soup

      4 cups cubed, peeled potatoes
      1 10½-ounce can condensed
            chicken broth
      1 cup thinly sliced celery
      ½ cup chopped carrot
      ½ cup chopped onion
      2 tablespoons snipped parsley
    1½ teaspoons salt
      ⅛ teaspoon pepper
            Dash dillweed
      1 tablespoon chopped canned
            pimiento (optional)
    3½ cups milk
      3 tablespoons all-purpose flour
      ½ cup milk
      2 tablespoons butter or margarine

In 3-quart saucepan combine first 9 ingredients. Bring to boiling; reduce heat. Cover and simmer till vegetables are tender, about 15 to 20 minutes. Add pimiento and the 3½ cups milk. Heat soup just till milk is hot. Blend flour with the ½ cup milk; stir into soup. Cook, stirring constantly, till thickened and bubbly. Add butter or margarine. Makes 6 to 8 servings.

Gourmet Potato Soup

      3 cups diced potato
      ½ cup diced celery
      ½ cup diced onion
      1 tablespoon chicken-flavored
            gravy base *or* 2 chicken
            boullion cubes
      2 cups milk
      1 8-ounce carton sour cream dip
            with chives (1 cup)
      1 tablespoon all-purpose flour

In large saucepan combine potato, celery, onion, 1½ cups water, gravy base, and ¼ teaspoon salt. Cover and cook till vegetables are tender, about 20 minutes. Add *1 cup* milk; heat through. In medium bowl blend sour cream dip and flour; gradually stir in remaining milk.

Pour about *one-third* of hot potato mixture into sour cream mixture; return to saucepan. Cook and stir till thickened. Garnish with parsley, if desired. Makes 6 to 8 servings.

Potato flavor can be added to various types of breads—loaves, rolls, and doughnuts—and is usually achieved by adding mashed potatoes to the recipe formula. Leftover or instant mashed potatoes are perfectly suited for this use.

Potato Rolls

Serve warm and fragrant right from the oven—

      1 package active dry yeast
      4 to 4½ cups sifted all-purpose
            flour
            • • •
    1¼ cups milk
      ¼ cup shortening
      ¼ cup sugar
    1½ teaspoons salt
      ½ cup hot mashed potatoes
            • • •
      1 egg

In large mixer bowl combine yeast and *2 cups* flour. Heat milk, shortening, sugar, and salt just till warm, stirring occasionally to melt shortening; stir in the potatoes.

Add to dry mixture in mixer bowl; add egg. Beat at low speed of electric mixer for ½ minute, scraping sides of bowl constantly. Beat 3 minutes at high speed. By hand, stir in enough remaining flour to make a soft dough. Knead on lightly floured surface till smooth and elastic, about 6 to 8 minutes.

Place in lightly greased bowl, turning once to grease surface. Cover; let rise till double, about 1 hour. Punch down. Shape in ball. Cover and let rest 10 minutes. Shape in rolls; place on greased baking sheet. Let rise till almost double, about 1 hour. Bake at 400° for 10 to 12 minutes. Cool on rack. Makes 2 dozen.

Men, women, and children alike are meat-and-potato fans. Use this combination as the basis for meal-in-one casseroles, stews, and other main dish recipes.

Ham-Stuffed Potatoes

4 large baking potatoes
2 cups ground fully cooked ham
1 cup mayonnaise or salad dressing
2 ounces process Swiss cheese, shredded (½ cup)
2 tablespoons chopped green pepper
2 tablespoons chopped canned pimiento
1 tablespoon instant minced onion
1 ounce process American cheese, shredded (¼ cup)

Scrub potatoes. Bake at 425° till done, about 45 to 60 minutes. Cut slice from top of each. Scoop out insides and cube. Toss with ham and next 5 ingredients; spoon into potato shells. Bake at 425° for 15 minutes. Sprinkle American cheese atop. Heat till cheese melts, about 1 to 2 minutes more. Makes 4 servings.

Sausage au Gratin

Reserve 3 links from one 12-ounce package smoked sausage links (8 links); slice remaining and set aside. Beat together one 8-ounce jar process cheese spread (1 cup) and 1 cup dairy sour cream till mixture is smooth. Add 1 tablespoon instant minced onion, 2 teaspoons dry parsley flakes, and ½ teaspoon salt.

Fold into 6 cups sliced, peeled, cooked potatoes (about 6 medium) with sliced sausages. Turn into a 1½-quart casserole. Bake the mixture at 350° for 40 minutes. Cut reserved sausages in half; arrange them atop the casserole in pinwheel-fashion. Bake till the sausages are heated through and the mixture is hot, about 10 minutes more. Makes 6 servings.

Hale and hearty

← Ladle liberal helpings of this vegetable-laden Potato Soup. Vibrant carrots, celery, and a hint of dillweed flatter each serving.

Lamb-Vegetable Supper

2 pounds boneless lamb, cut in cubes
3 tablespoons all-purpose flour
¼ cup salad oil
1 teaspoon salt
¼ teaspoon pepper
¼ teaspoon dried thyme leaves, crushed
¼ teaspoon dried basil leaves, crushed
1 clove garlic, minced
1 whole bay leaf
1 cup water
⅓ cup dry white wine
• • •
4 medium potatoes, peeled and cut up (3 cups)
2 onions, quartered
2 tomatoes, quartered

Coat lamb with flour; brown in hot oil. Sprinkle with salt and pepper. Add thyme, basil, garlic, bay leaf, water, and wine. Cover; simmer 30 minutes. Add the potato and onion. Sprinkle lightly with additional salt.

Cover; cook till vegetables are tender, about 30 minutes more. Add tomatoes. Cover; cook till heated through, 2 to 3 minutes. Remove bay leaf before serving. Makes 6 servings.

Turkey-Potato Pancakes

Make after the holidays with leftover turkey—

3 beaten eggs
3 cups shredded raw potato, drained (about 3 potatoes)
1½ cups finely chopped turkey
1½ teaspoons grated onion
Dash pepper
1 tablespoon all-purpose flour
1½ teaspoons salt

In mixing bowl combine eggs, potato, turkey, onion, and pepper. Add flour and salt; mix well. Using about ¼ cup batter for each pancake, drop batter onto hot, greased griddle, spreading to about 4 inches in diameter. Cook over medium-low heat for 3 to 4 minutes on each side. Serve the pancakes with cranberry sauce, if desired. Makes about 15 pancakes.

Potato shells hold a fluffy potato, blue cheese, and sour cream combo. Garnish Blue Cheese-Bacon Potatoes with bacon.

Chuck Wagon Stew

Cut 2 pounds lean beef chuck in 1½-inch cubes. In Dutch oven brown the meat slowly in 2 tablespoons hot shortening. Add 2 cups water;* 1 medium onion, sliced; 1 clove garlic, minced; 1 tablespoon salt; 1 teaspoon sugar; ¼ teaspoon dried thyme leaves, crushed; and 1 teaspoon Worcestershire sauce. Cover the mixture; simmer about 1½ hours, stirring occasionally to prevent the meat from sticking.

Add ½ cup celery, sliced in ½-inch pieces; 6 carrots, cut in 1-inch slices; ½ pound small white onions *or* one 16-ounce can onions, drained; and 3 potatoes, peeled and quartered. Cook, covered, for 20 minutes. Add 2 or 3 tomatoes, cut in wedges *or* one 16-ounce can tomatoes, drained (reserve liquid). Cook till the meat and the vegetables are tender, about 15 minutes. Skim fat from the stew. Thicken liquid with flour, if desired. Makes 6 to 8 servings. *If canned tomatoes are used, use the drained juice as part of the liquid.

Monday Meat Pie

  ½ cup chopped onion
  1 tablespoon shortening
  2 to 3 cups cooked beef, cut in
      ½-inch cubes
  2 cups cubed, peeled, cooked
      potatoes
  2 medium carrots, cooked and
      sliced (1 cup)
  4 ounces sharp process American
      cheese, shredded (1 cup)
  ½ cup mayonnaise or salad dressing
  1 10¾-ounce can beef gravy
      (1¼ cups)
  1 14-ounce package corn bread mix

Cook the ½ cup chopped onion in hot shortening till tender but not brown. Add beef, potatoes, carrots, *half* the cheese, mayonnaise, and gravy. Heat to boiling; pour into a 9x9x2-inch baking dish. Prepare corn bread mix according to package directions, adding remaining cheese. Spoon over meat mixture. Bake at 400° for 25 minutes. Makes 6 to 8 servings.

Meat and Potato Balls

  1 beaten egg
  2 tablespoons milk
  ¼ cup fine dry bread crumbs
  1 cup finely shredded, peeled, raw
      potato, drained (1 large)
  ¼ cup chopped green onion with
      tops
  1 teaspoon prepared mustard
  1 pound ground pork
  2 tablespoons shortening
  1 chicken bouillon cube
  2 tablespoons all-purpose flour

Combine first 6 ingredients, ¾ teaspoon salt, and ⅛ teaspoon pepper. Add pork; mix well. Shape into 24 meatballs. In skillet brown meatballs in hot shortening; drain off fat. Dissolve bouillon cube in 1 cup boiling water; add to meatballs. Cover and cook over low heat for 20 minutes, turning occasionally.

Remove meatballs to serving bowl; reserve pan drippings. Blend flour with ⅓ cup cold water; stir into reserved drippings. Cook and stir till thick and bubbly. Serve with meatballs. Makes 4 to 6 servings.

The summer picnic favorite, potato salad, has been adapted to fit many different tastes. Hot or cold, cubed or mashed, potatoes are accompanied by vegetables varying in texture, flavor, and color. Coat with a creamy mayonnaise dressing, piquant sour cream blend, or tangy vinegar-oil mixture according to preference.

Potluck Potato Salad

¼ cup clear French salad dressing
    with spices and herbs
4 to 5 medium potatoes, cooked,
    peeled, and cubed (4 cups)
1 cup chopped celery
¼ cup chopped onion
4 hard-cooked eggs, sliced
1 teaspoon salt
½ cup mayonnaise

Pour French dressing over warm potatoes; chill 2 hours. Add celery, onion, eggs, and salt. Add mayonnaise to the mixture and mix carefully. Stir in 1 teaspoon celery seed, if desired. Chill about 4 hours. Makes 8 servings.

Calico Potato Salad

6 cups diced, peeled, cooked
    potatoes
½ cup diced cucumber
½ cup chopped onion
¼ cup chopped green pepper
3 tablespoons chopped canned
    pimiento
1½ teaspoons salt
¾ teaspoon celery seed
¼ teaspoon pepper
2 hard-cooked eggs
½ cup whipping cream, whipped
½ cup mayonnaise
2 tablespoons vinegar
1 tablespoon prepared mustard

Combine first 8 ingredients. Coarsely chop eggs, reserving 1 whole egg yolk. Add chopped eggs to potato mixture. Chill. Combine remaining ingredients, *except* yolk; toss with potato mixture ½ hour before serving. To serve, spoon into lettuce-lined bowl. Sieve reserved yolk over. Makes 10 to 12 servings.

Peppy Potato Salad

¼ teaspoon mustard seed
¼ teaspoon dillseed
1 tablespoon water
1½ cups diced, peeled, cooked
    potatoes
1 tablespoon sliced green onion
2 tablespoons thinly sliced celery
1 hard-cooked egg, chopped
¼ cup Zippy Cooked Dressing

Soak mustard seed and dillseed in water several hours or overnight. Combine seed-water mixture and ½ teaspoon salt. Add potatoes, onion, and celery; mix lightly. Add egg and ¼ cup Zippy Cooked Dressing; toss to coat. Chill thoroughly. Garnish with radish roses, if desired. Serves 2.

Zippy Cooked Dressing: In a small saucepan mix together 1 tablespoon all-purpose flour, 1 tablespoon sugar, ½ teaspoon salt, ½ teaspoon dry mustard, and dash cayenne. Gradually stir in 1 slightly beaten egg yolk and ⅓ cup milk. Cook and stir over medium heat till mixture is thickened and bubbly. Remove from heat; stir in 2 tablespoons vinegar and 1 teaspoon butter. Cover; cool. Makes ½ cup.

Note: Make Thousand Island dressing from remaining cooked dressing, stirring in 1 tablespoon chili sauce and 1 teaspoon pickle relish; serve over lettuce another time.

Hot Dill-Potato Salad

1 tablespoon butter or margarine
1 tablespoon all-purpose flour
1 teaspoon salt
¼ teaspoon dried dillweed
⅛ teaspoon pepper
1 cup milk
½ cup mayonnaise or salad
    dressing
2 tablespoons finely chopped onion
4 cups diced, peeled, cooked
    potatoes
Paprika

In saucepan melt butter over low heat. Stir in flour, salt, dillweed, and pepper. Add milk; cook and stir till thickened and bubbly. Blend in mayonnaise and onion; fold in potatoes. Heat through. Spoon into serving dish; sprinkle with paprika. Serve at once. Serves 4 to 6.

German Potato Salad

　½ pound bacon (10 to 12 slices)
　½ cup chopped onion
　2 tablespoons all-purpose flour
　2 tablespoons sugar
1½ teaspoons salt
　1 teaspoon celery seed
　　Dash pepper
　1 cup water
　½ cup vinegar
　　•　•　•
　6 cups sliced, peeled,
　　　cooked potatoes
　2 hard-cooked eggs, sliced
　　　(optional)
　　Parsley
　　Chopped canned pimiento
　　Bacon curls

Cook bacon till it is crisp; drain and crumble the bacon, reserving ¼ cup fat. Cook onion in the reserved fat till the onion is tender. Blend in flour, sugar, salt, celery seed, and pepper. Add water and vinegar; cook and stir till the mixture is thickened and bubbly. Add bacon, potatoes, and eggs; heat thoroughly, tossing lightly. Garnish with parsley, pimiento, and bacon curls. Makes 8 to 10 servings.

Ham and Potato Salad

　2 cups cubed, peeled, cooked
　　　potatoes
　1 tablespoon Italian salad
　　　dressing
1½ cups cubed fully cooked ham
　2 hard-cooked eggs, chopped
　½ cup diced unpeeled cucumber
　¼ cup sliced radishes
　¼ cup chopped celery
　2 tablespoons chopped onion
　2 tablespoons chopped green
　　　pepper
　¼ teaspoon salt
　⅛ teaspoon paprika
　½ cup mayonnaise

Sprinkle cubed potatoes with Italian dressing. Let stand for ½ hour. Add the remaining ingredients, *except* mayonnaise, to the potatoes. Chill the mixture thoroughly. Before serving, gently fold in mayonnaise. Makes 5 servings.

Potato products: Supermarket shelves and freezer cases are lined with various prepared potato products to tempt you into enjoying potatoes with time saving ease. Their increasing popularity has reduced the cost per serving, making them almost comparable in cost to fresh potatoes.

Potato chips are very thin slices of potato that are fried to crisp goodness, then salted. Seventy percent of all processed potatoes are utilized in this manner. Their popularity as a snack, appetizer, or sandwich accompaniment is a well recognized fact. Crushed potato chips also serve occasionally as a recipe ingredient.

Crunchy Ham Sandwiches

Add sliced cheese and tomato, coat with crushed potato chips, and grill—

　8 slices white bread
　　Butter or margarine, softened
　　Prepared mustard
　4 slices boiled ham
　4 slices process American cheese
　1 tomato, thinly sliced
　　•　•　•
　2 slightly beaten eggs
　2 tablespoons milk
　　Dash onion salt
1¼ cups crushed potato chips

Spread 4 slices bread on one side with butter; spread remaining bread slices on one side with mustard. Top each mustard-spread slice with 1 slice ham, 1 slice cheese, and 1 or 2 slices tomato, then with second slice of bread.

Combine eggs, milk, and onion salt. Dip sandwiches in egg mixture, then in crushed potato chips. Pat to secure chips to bread, turning to coat both sides. Brown the sandwiches on both sides in a buttered skillet or on a lightly greased griddle till crisp, about 8 minutes. Serve the sandwiches hot. Serves 4.

For a potluck supper

Bring a bowlful of Calico Potato Salad gar- →
nished with sieved egg yolk and lined with green onion, ham, and cheese roll-ups.

Canned potatoes include small, whole potatoes as well as sliced potatoes and plain as well as dressed-up versions. Shoestring potatoes are short potato strips that have been crisp-fried and salted like potato chips. They have the advantage over potato chips of being shelf stable. Canned potato salads are also produced.

Hot Potato Salad Fix-Up

Brings out the best in canned potato salad—

- 2 16-ounce cans German-style potato salad
- 8 slices bacon, crisp-cooked, drained, and coarsely crumbled
- 4 ounces sharp process American cheese, diced (1 cup)

Combine all of the ingredients in a 1½-quart casserole. Bake the mixture, uncovered, in a 300° oven for about 25 to 30 minutes. Serve the potato salad hot. Makes 6 servings.

Dehydrated potatoes permit the jiffy preparation of some of the most popular potato dishes using instant mashed potato granules and flakes, hashed brown potato mixes, and potato casserole mixes.

Creamy Potato Bake

Omitting the butter, prepare 6 servings instant mashed potatoes according to package directions. Add one 4-ounce carton whipped cream cheese; beat well. Stir in 1 beaten egg, 2 tablespoons finely chopped green onion, and 1 tablespoon finely snipped parsley; blend well.

Transfer the mixture to a well-greased 1-quart baking dish. Dot with 1 tablespoon butter. Sprinkle with paprika. Bake at 400° for about 40 minutes. Makes 6 servings.

Just for two

Peppy Potato Salad is a scaled-down salad for the twosome to enjoy. Colorful radish roses and romaine leaves crown the salad.

Potato Clouds

    Packaged instant mashed potatoes
        (enough for 4 servings)
2 slightly beaten egg yolks
2 teaspoons snipped parsley
2 teaspoons instant minced onion
¼ cup sifted all-purpose flour
1 teaspoon baking powder
2 stiff-beaten egg whites

Prepare instant mashed potatoes according to package directions; cool. Stir in egg yolks, parsley, and onion. Sift together flour, baking powder, and ½ teaspoon salt. Add to potato mixture; mix well. Fold in egg whites.

Drop by rounded tablespoons into deep hot fat (385°). Cook till puffs of potato are brown, turning once. Drain on absorbent towels. Keep hot in 300° oven while frying the remainder of the puffs. Makes about 2½ dozen.

Golden Potato Bake

Adding 1 teaspoon instant minced onion to cooking water, prepare enough packaged instant mashed potatoes to make 4 servings, according to package directions. Fold in 1 cup cubed cooked carrots. Spoon the mixture into 4 individual casserole dishes. Top each casserole dish with 1 tablespoon grated Parmesan cheese. Bake the casseroles at 350° till they are golden brown, about 25 minutes. Makes 4 servings.

Double Potato Bake

    Packaged dry hashed brown
        potatoes (enough for 4 servings)
1 10½-ounce can condensed cream
    of potato soup
1 soup can milk
1 tablespoon instant minced onion
1 tablespoon snipped parsley
⅓ cup grated Parmesan cheese

Prepare potatoes according to package directions, reducing cooking time to 11 or 12 minutes; drain. Combine soup, milk, onion, parsley, and dash pepper. Heat soup mixture. Add to potatoes; mix lightly. Turn into a 10x6x1¾-inch baking dish. Sprinkle with cheese. Bake at 350° for 35 minutes. Serves 6.

Frozen potatoes also come in a wide variety of shapes and styles. Many-shaped French fries, hashed browns, nuggets, and puffs are only a few of the products. These require only minimal heating in an oven or skillet. (See also *Sweet Potato, Vegetable, Yam* for additional information.)

Creamy Hashed Brown Bake

So quick, yet so good—

1 10½-ounce can condensed cream
    of celery soup
⅓ cup milk
1 3-ounce package cream cheese
        •   •   •
4 cups loose-pack, frozen hashed
    brown potatoes
1 8-ounce can small whole onions,
    drained and cut in pieces
        •   •   •
2 ounces sharp process American
    cheese, shredded (½ cup)

In saucepan combine celery soup, milk, and cream cheese; cook and stir over medium heat till ingredients are smooth. Combine frozen hashed brown potatoes and canned onions; stir in soup mixture. Pour into a 10x6x1¾-inch baking dish; cover with foil. Bake at 350° till the potatoes are tender, about 1¼ hours. Remove foil; top with shredded process cheese. Return to oven until the cheese melts. Serves 6.

POTATO FLOUR or STARCH—Dried and ground potato used by itself as a thickener or in combination with wheat flour for breads and baked goods. When used for thickening, one-half tablespoon potato flour produces the same thickness as one tablespoon of wheat flour. (See also *Flour.*)

POTATO PANCAKE—The English translation of the German phrase *Kartoffel Pfannkuchen*, a dish made with grated raw potato. (See also *Kartoffel Pfannkuchen.*)

POT-AU-FEU (*pô tō foe'*)—A French phrase that literally means "pot on the fire," but which traditionally refers to a rich soup or stew made with meat and vegetables.

POT CHEESE—A soft, unripened cheese that is similar to cottage cheese. In fact, cottage cheese is sometimes called pot cheese, although real pot cheese is drier.

POTHERB—1. An herb or plant cooked like a vegetable. 2. An herb used as a seasoning. Thyme, spinach, and wild greens are herbs and plants used as potherbs.

POT LIQUOR, POTLIKKER, or POTLICKER—The liquid that remains after meat, such as salt pork or bacon, and/or vegetables, such as greens, have been cooked in a large amount of water.

Pot liquor is mainly associated with southern and Afro-American cookery. Corn bread is a favorite combination with this broth. (See also *Regional Cookery*.)

POTPIE—A deep-dish pie or stew made with meat or poultry, vegetables, and a biscuit, dumpling, or pastry topping. The Pennsylvania Dutch also use noodles in potpies.

Potpies are a favorite with homemakers because all kinds of leftovers as well as newly purchased ingredients can be used in them. Just save those dabs of cooked vegetables and combine all of them with chunks of cooked meat to create a new dish. Make the topping from scratch if you like, or use mixes or refrigerated biscuits.

There is also a large selection of frozen potpies in the supermarkets that you can keep on hand for quick meals.

Chicken Potpie

  1 3-pound ready-to-cook stewing chicken, cut up
  1 medium onion, quartered
  3 celery leaves
  3 sprigs parsley
  1 bay leaf
10 whole black peppercorns
¼ teaspoon dried rosemary leaves, crushed
  1 10-ounce package frozen peas
  7 carrots, peeled and cut up
¼ cup all-purpose flour
½ cup milk
   Plain Pastry (See *Pastry*) for 1-crust pie

In large kettle combine chicken, onion, celery leaves, parsley, bay leaf, peppercorns, and rosemary. Add 2 quarts water and 2 teaspoons salt. Bring to boiling; simmer, covered, till chicken is tender, about 2 hours. Meanwhile, thaw peas. Remove chicken from broth. Strain stock. In 2 cups of the stock, cook carrots, covered, till tender. Remove chicken from bones; cube. Turn into 2-quart casserole.

Blend flour, 1 teaspoon salt, and dash pepper with milk. Stir quickly into stock with carrots. Add thawed peas. Bring to boiling, stirring constantly. Simmer till peas are tender. Pour over chicken in casserole; toss.

Roll pastry to fit top of casserole with ½-inch overhang. Turn edge under; seal and crimp. Slash vents in top. Bake at 425° for about 20 minutes. Makes 6 to 8 servings.

Tamale Pie

  1 pound ground beef
  1 cup chopped onion
  1 cup chopped green pepper
  2 8-ounce cans tomato sauce
  1 12-ounce can whole kernel corn, drained
½ cup pitted ripe olives, chopped
  1 clove garlic, minced
  1 tablespoon sugar
  1 teaspoon salt
  2 to 3 teaspoons chili powder
   Dash pepper
  6 ounces sharp process American cheese, shredded (1½ cups)
¾ cup yellow cornmeal
½ teaspoon salt
  2 cups cold water
  1 tablespoon butter or margarine

In large skillet cook ground beef, onion, and green pepper till meat is lightly browned and vegetables are tender. Stir in tomato sauce, corn, olives, garlic, sugar, the 1 teaspoon salt, chili powder, and pepper. Simmer till mixture is thick, about 20 to 25 minutes. Add shredded cheese; stir till melted. Turn into a well-greased 9x9x2-inch baking dish.

To make cornmeal topping, stir cornmeal and ½ teaspoon salt into cold water. Cook, stirring constantly, till thick. Add butter or margarine; mix well. Spoon over hot meat mixture. Bake at 375° about 40 minutes. Serves 6.

Kidney-Vegetable Pie

  1 beef kidney
  4 cups water
  1 tablespoon salt
  1 pound beef stew meat, cut in
     ½-inch cubes
  ¼ cup all-purpose flour
  2 tablespoons shortening
1½ cups tomato juice
  1 cup water
  1 medium onion, sliced
1¼ teaspoons salt
  ¼ teaspoon dried thyme, crushed

      • • •

  3 medium carrots, sliced
  3 stalks celery, sliced
  1 10-ounce package frozen lima beans
     or one 16-ounce can green lima
     beans, drained
  2 tablespoons cold water
  1 tablespoon all-purpose flour
    Pastry Topper

Remove membrane and hard parts from the beef kidney. In saucepan combine kidney, 4 cups water, and 1 tablespoon salt. Soak for 1 hour; drain kidney. Cover with cold water. Bring to boiling; simmer, covered, 20 minutes. Drain; cut kidney in ½-inch cubes.

Coat stew meat with ¼ cup flour. In Dutch oven brown stew meat in hot shortening. Add tomato juice, 1 cup water, onion, 1¼ teaspoons salt, and thyme; cover and simmer till meat is almost tender, about 1 hour. Stir in carrots, celery, and lima beans; simmer, covered, till vegetables are tender, 30 minutes longer. Add kidney; bring mixture to boiling. Combine 2 tablespoons cold water and 1 tablespoon flour; stir into stew. Cook and stir till thickened and bubbly. Pour into 2-quart casserole. Place Pastry Topper atop *hot* mixture. Bake at 450° till pastry is lightly browned, about 15 to 20 minutes. Makes 6 servings.

Pastry Topper: Sift together 1½ cups sifted all-purpose flour and ½ teaspon salt. Cut in ½ cup shortening till pieces are the size of small peas. Sprinkle 1 tablespoon cold water over part of mixture; gently toss with fork. Repeat with additional 3 to 4 tablespoons cold water till all mixture is moistened. Form into ball. Roll out on lightly floured surface to 8-inch circle, ¼ inch thick. Cut pastry in 6 pie-shaped wedges; prick with fork.

Savory Chicken Pies

  ½ pound bulk pork sausage
  ¼ cup butter or margarine
  ⅓ cup all-purpose flour
  1 13¾-ounce can chicken broth
  ⅔ cup milk
  2 cups cubed, cooked chicken
  1 10-ounce package frozen peas,
     thawed
    Savory Pastry

In saucepan brown sausage, breaking into pieces; drain on paper toweling. Pour off fat. In same saucepan melt butter or margarine. Blend in flour, ¼ teaspoon salt, and ⅛ teaspoon pepper. Stir in chicken broth and milk. Cook and stir till thickened and bubbly; cook 1 minute more. Add browned sausage, cubed chicken, and thawed peas; heat through. Divide mixture among six 1-cup casseroles. Top with Savory Pastry. Place casseroles on baking sheet. Bake at 425° for 25 to 30 minutes. Serves 6.

Savory Pastry: Combine 1 cup sifted all-purpose flour, 1 teaspoon celery seed, ½ teaspoon salt, and ½ teaspoon paprika; cut in ⅓ cup shortening. Sprinkle with 2 tablespoons water, a tablespoon at a time, mixing with fork till all flour is moistened and dough clings together. Gather dough together; press into ball. Roll ⅛ inch thick on the lightly floured surface. Cut into 6 circles the size of the casseroles. Cut slits near center of circles; place one pastry circle on top of each casserole.

Clam Chowder Casserole

Cook two 10-ounce packages frozen cauliflower according to package directions. Drain well; cut up large pieces. In saucepan cook ½ cup chopped onion and ½ cup chopped celery in ¼ cup butter till tender but not brown. Blend in ¼ cup all-purpose flour, ¾ teaspoon salt, and ⅛ teaspoon pepper. Add 2 cups milk and 1 chicken bouillon cube. Cook and stir till thickened and bubbly. Add cauliflower; two 7½-ounce cans minced clams, drained; and 2 tablespoons chopped canned pimiento. Heat to boiling. Turn into 2-quart casserole. Brush 1 package refrigerated biscuits (6) with 2 tablespoons melted butter; sprinkle with 2 tablespoons grated Parmesan cheese. Halve; place atop *hot* mixture. Bake at 450° for 15 minutes. Serves 6.

POT ROAST–1. A large piece of meat, usually beef, that is cooked by braising. **2.** A term meaning to braise meat or poultry in a "pot" with a cover, which includes a Dutch oven, covered skillet, or a foil wrap.

Any type of meat or poultry can be pot roasted (braised). The less-tender beef cuts, such as chuck, blade, and arm pot roasts, are well suited to this method of cooking. Occasionally, lamb, pork, veal, variety meats, and poultry are braised, too.

The procedure for pot-roasting begins with browning the meat in fat. This develops the brown color and the flavor that appeal to many people. The meat may or may not be coated with flour for browning. Water, tomato juice, diluted soy sauce, broth, cider, or wine is added for the long, slow cooking, which tenderizes the meat. The pot roast is simmered, tightly covered, in this liquid for several hours.

During the last hour of cooking, vegetables are quite often added. This is sometimes referred to as a Yankee pot roast. Onions, carrots, potatoes, tomatoes, and turnips are among the vegetables that are used alone or in combinations. Once the meat and vegetables are tender, the juices are made into a gravy that is served with the roast. (See also *Beef*.)

Beef Pot Roast

Coat one 3- to 4-pound beef pot roast with flour. In Dutch oven, large skillet, or roasting pan, brown slowly on all sides in 2 tablespoons hot shortening or salad oil. Season with salt and pepper. Remove from heat; add ½ cup water *or* beef broth. Cover; simmer till tender, 2½ hours. Add water, if needed.

If desired, add small potatoes, peeled and halved; small whole onions; and medium carrots, peeled and cut in 1-inch pieces, the last 45 to 60 minutes. Using pan juices, prepare Pot Roast Gravy (See *Gravy*). Serves 6 to 8.

All-American favorites

⊢ Simmering the meat and vegetables together makes Yankee Pot Roast what it is — a hearty, wholesome dish with great flavor.

Pot Roast Variations

Use tomato juice instead of the ½ cup water for the cooking liquid in Beef Pot Roast. Thicken the juices for Pot Roast Gravy (See *Gravy*), *except* use tomato juice instead of water and use only 3 tablespoons all-purpose flour. Season the pot roast with salt, pepper, and ½ teaspoon Worcestershire sauce.

Cook Beef Pot Roast, slicing 2 small onions over meat after browning. Add 2 bay leaves and 5 whole cloves. Use ¼ cup vinegar and ¼ cup water as the cooking liquid for the roast.

After browning, season Beef Pot Roast with salt, pepper, and 1 tablespoon dillseed. Top meat with 2 medium onions, sliced. Serve roast with Sour Cream Gravy (See *Gravy*).

Mix one 8-ounce can tomato sauce, 1 cup water, 1 envelope *dry* onion soup mix, 1 teaspoon caraway seed, and 2 bay leaves. Pour the mixture over Beef Pot Roast after browning. Thicken liquid as for Pot Roast Gravy, *using only* 2 tablespoons all-purpose flour.

Yankee Pot Roast

Select a 3- to 4-pound chuck roast. Trim off excess fat; heat trimmings in Dutch oven or large skillet. When there are about 2 tablespoons melted fat, remove trimmings. Coat pot roast with flour; brown slowly on both sides in hot fat. Season with salt and pepper.

Add ½ cup water. Cover tightly and cook over low heat till tender, 2½ to 3 hours. Add more water, if needed. The last hour of cooking, add small whole onions, peeled carrots, and peeled small potatoes. Place meat on platter; surround with vegetables. Garnish with fresh celery leaves. Make Yankee Pot Roast Gravy, if desired. Makes 6 to 8 servings.

Yankee Pot Roast Gravy: Skim most of fat from pan juices. Reserve 1½ to 2 cups stock. Put ½ cup cold water into a shaker or small screw-top jar, and then add ¼ cup all-purpose flour. Shake to mix thoroughly.

Remove stock from heat and slowly stir in flour mixture. Return to heat and cook, stirring constantly, till gravy is bubbling vigorously. Season to taste with salt and pepper. Cook about 5 minutes more, stirring constantly.

Savory Blade Pot Roast

Simmering meat in an herb-seasoned liquid tenderizes and flavors the roast—

    1 **3-pound blade-bone pot roast**
      Salad oil
      Salt
    ¼ **cup wine vinegar**
    ¼ **cup salad oil**
    ¼ **cup catsup**
    2 **tablespoons soy sauce**
    2 **tablespoons Worcestershire sauce**
    1 **teaspoon dried rosemary leaves, crushed**
    ½ **teaspoon garlic powder**
    ½ **teaspoon dry mustard**

In skillet or Dutch oven brown meat slowly in a small amount of hot salad oil. Sprinkle meat with salt. Combine wine vinegar, the ¼ cup salad oil, catsup, soy sauce, Worcestershire sauce, dried rosemary, garlic powder, and dry mustard. Pour mixture over meat. Cover tightly and simmer till tender, about 2 hours.

Remove pot roast to a heated platter. Skim excess fat from pan juices; spoon juices over meat, Or, if desired, make Pot Roast Gravy to serve with roast (see *Gravy*). Serves 6 to 8.

POTS AND PANS—Containers that hold food during cooking. The category of pots and pans ranges from skillets and saucepans to baking pans and pressure cookers. The distinction between the two is that pans are used on top of the range and almost always have one handle, while pots have two handles. Many pots and pans are available in two forms—as a standard utensil and as a small electrical appliance.

Pots and pans were one of the earliest inventions of man. Needing something in which to cook food, he fashioned crude pots out of clay, reeds, and mud.

Once man learned how to work metal, he used this skill not only to make weapons but also to make utensils in which to cook his food. By the beginning of the Christian Era, the Romans, as surviving records show, had an amazing number of cooking utensils. In addition to the many earthenware vessels, they had a type of saucepan, kettles that could be suspended over a fire,

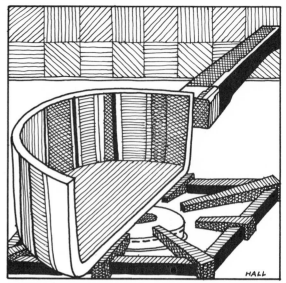

Selecting a good pot or pan will make cooking easier. Be sure the pan is balanced, has a flat bottom, and has straight sides.

a grill-like unit for broiling meat, a handled frying pan, and a double-bowled utensil that served the purpose a double boiler does today.

The settlers in America didn't fare so well. Although they had come from Europe where there were many cooking utensils, many pioneers had only a spit and an iron kettle suspended over the fire, and perhaps, a long-handled iron frypan called a spider with legs that sat over coals.

Today, however, the number and variety of pots and pans on the market dazzle the imagination. Some of these utensils are large; others are small. Some have multipurpose uses, while others fill specific needs. Therefore, you must choose pots and pans so that you will have the right utensil for the cooking job you want to do without taxing your budget or overloading the kitchen cabinets.

How to select: Whether you are a bride setting up your first kitchen, a career girl settling into an apartment, or an experienced homemaker replacing or adding to your basic kitchen equipment, consider these things when buying pots and pans: use, material, size, and design.

How the pot or pan is to be used is the first thing to consider when buying new equipment. Today, you can buy a pot or pan—from a common frypan and saucepan to the specialized springform pan and poele—to fill every basic and specialty cooking purpose. If possible, choose a pot or pan that can serve many purposes in the home. For instance, an attractive casserole acts as a baking and serving dish, a double boiler divides into two saucepans, and a Dutch oven substitutes for a large saucepan when equipment is limited.

Then, consider the type of material used in making the pot or pan, for each metal affects cooking performance, ease of cleaning, and appearance differently.

Aluminum is a good conductor of heat. Thus, foods cook evenly in aluminum pots and pans. These utensils will not rust, but they do turn dark when alkaline foods are cooked in them or when they are washed in dishwashers. This reaction is not harmful and can be removed by boiling a solution of water and vinegar or water and cream of tartar in the pot or pan or by polishing with a commercial polish.

Stainless steel is usually combined with another metal in pots and pans. A copper or aluminum layer over the bottom or sandwiched between two layers of stainless steel makes heat conduction even and prevents hot spots. Stainless steel maintains its beauty due to its high polish and its stain and scratch resistance.

Copper utensils are attractive and are excellent heat conductors. Because copper darkens with exposure to heat and air, it requires frequent polishing. It is used in combination with other metals.

Glass and glass ceramic react differently than do many other materials. They heat slowly but hold the heat well. Some glass utensils, such as baking dishes, are intended for cooking in the oven; others are intended for the top of the range. But some can go from the freezer to the oven. Read the label so that you will get the type that you need, and then use it only for the type of cooking that is specified by the manufacturer. Glass is not affected by food acids or alkalies. It is not hard to clean, but care must be taken in handling glass utensils so as not to scratch or break them.

Iron pots and pans, especially cast iron, are old favorites. These heavy utensils conduct and hold heat well. However, they will rust if not dried thoroughly.

Porcelain enamel and porcelain clad utensils are metal coated with a glass material. Not all of these conduct heat evenly. However, they do resist acids, alkalies, and rust. They're fairly easy to keep clean and are quite colorful, too.

Tin pots and pans are made by placing a tin coating over another metal such as steel. These utensils are lightweight and shiny when new. They can scratch, pit, and rust easily, though. Many of the small, light pots and pans such as egg poachers, pie pans, and bread pans are made of tin.

Many of the metal pans have a nonstick coating. This coating does not affect the taste of the food, but it does make the pan quite a bit easier to clean.

After you have decided on the use for the pot or pan and on which material you want, consider the size. Most pots and pans are a standard size, which the manufacturer marks on the bottom for easy reference. Saucepans are measured by volume; for example, one quart. Baking pans are grouped by dimensional measure. Baking pan sizes are measured across the top from one inside edge to the other.

Finally, consider the design. Good pots and pans have straight sides, a flat bottom for good contact with the heat, secure handles for convenience and safety, and tight-fitting lids. The handles and knobs on the lids are made of a heat-resistant material, so you can touch them without being burned and use them in the oven as well as on the top of the range.

Today, there is an abundance of attractive, gaily colored pots and pans on the market. Choose these for their charm as well as their serviceability, and they will not only help in cooking delicious foods easily, but they will also decorate the kitchen and brighten your tasks.

How to clean: Cleaning pots and pans correctly keeps them attractive and in good functioning condition. Always clean them thoroughly after each use. Any bits of stain or burned-on food will just be harder to remove the next time, so it's better to clean the pan completely the first time. Baking pans that are not completely clean bake less efficiently than those that are shiny and may make removal of the cooked food from them more difficult.

If you want to soak a pot or pan to loosen any stain or food, always wait until the pan has had a chance to cool before adding water. Putting cold water into a hot pan can cause warping. This damages the future performance of the pan—a warped pan will not heat evenly.

Soaking is especially good for cleaning glass and porcelain enamel, which can scratch if scoured. Metals can be scoured if you note the manufacturer's directions and use mild products when specified. There are special cleaners and polishes sold for some metals, which make the pots and pans sparkle with less work.

How to store: Storing pots and pans correctly will make them easier to reach and will also prevent denting or breaking.

Treat everyone to a dessert that looks as enchanting as it tastes. The tiny cups not only look attractive, but they also keep servings of rich Pots de Crème Chocolate small.

Stack pie plates, cake pans, and muffin tins in graduating sizes to conserve space. Lay cookie sheets flat or stand them on end. Large, bulky items that are not used frequently, such as tube pans, should be stored out of the way so that most-used pots and pans are easier to get out and won't be scraped and dented in the shuffle.

Pots and pans that have a nonstick coating should be handled with care so that the finish is not scarred. Protect them from sharp corners or edges that might scratch the surface and damage the finish.

Taking care of pots and pans serves two purposes: it adds years of use, and it is economical. (See *Equipment*, individual metals for additional information.)

POTS DE CRÈME (*pō duh krem'*)— A custardlike dessert served in small cups. Pots de crème is rich and is usually chocolate- but sometimes vanilla- or caramel-flavored. The pudding is served cold, with or without a dollop of whipped cream.

Pots de crème is traditionally served in small cups made especially for this dessert. However, if you do not have a pots de crème set, you can serve the smooth pudding in sherbet glasses or in tiny bowls. The dessert is very rich, so only a small amount of it should be served to each person. (See also *Dessert*.)

Pots de Crème Chocolate

Make this creamy dessert in a jiffy by using a combination of convenience products—

    2¼ cups milk
    1 4-ounce package *regular*
        chocolate pudding mix
    1 6-ounce package semisweet
        chocolate pieces (1 cup)
    1 teaspoon vanilla
        Pressurized dessert topping

Using the 2¼ cups milk, prepare pudding mix according to package directions. While pudding is hot, add semisweet chocolate pieces. Stir till melted; cool. Add vanilla and beat till smooth. Spoon into pot de crème cups and chill. Before serving, garnish with swirl of pressurized dessert topping. Makes 6 servings.

Pots de Crème

A classic chocolate dessert—

    1 6-ounce package semisweet
        chocolate pieces
    1¼ cups light cream
    2 egg yolks
        Dash salt

In heavy saucepan combine chocolate pieces and light cream. Stir over low heat till blended and satin-smooth. Mixture should be *slightly thick but not boiling*. Beat egg yolks and salt till airy and thick. Gradually stir in hot chocolate mixture. Spoon into 6 or 7 pot de crème cups or small sherbets. Cover; chill till of pudding consistency, about 3 hours.

POTTED CHEESE—A mixture of finely grated cheese and seasonings. Cheddar cheese usually forms the foundation, with butter, condiments, spirits, vinegar, salt, and coloring added in various combinations. Sometimes a smoke flavor is added. These flavors go well with toast or crackers.

Commercial potted cheese comes in glass jars or in small crocks with tight-fitting lids. Either the commercial or the homemade cheese makes a nice gift, especially around the Christmas season.

POTTED MEAT—Meat ground to a paste and mixed with seasonings. Potted meats are available in small cans, or you can make your own by using a food grinder or an electric blender. The meat makes good sandwich fillings and appetizer spreads.

POUCHONG TEA (*pōo' chong'*)—A type of oolong tea that usually comes from Formosa. The tea is scented with blossoms of jasmine or gardenia (See also *Tea*.)

POULET (*pōo lā'*)—A French word for chicken, especially a young chicken.

POULETTE SAUCE (*pōo let'*)—A velouté sauce with meat or fish stock, egg yolk, onion, lemon juice, and occasionally mushrooms added for additional flavor. This velvety sauce goes with chicken, fish, eggs, and various kinds of vegetables.

# POULTRY

Make every week seem like the holidays by using these modern techniques for cooking poultry.

At one time, poultry flew free as wild game. When man domesticated this wild game, he provided himself with an abundant supply of meat and eggs: chicken, turkey, duck, goose, and guinea fowl.

The first "breeding program" began about 4000 years ago when the jungle fowl in and around India were domesticated. Later, Greeks and Romans developed poultry farms. The birds raised in Greece and Rome furnished not only meat and eggs but also a few fringe benefits. On one occasion, geese are said to have saved Rome by warning its inhabitants of approaching enemies. Because of this, geese were rewarded with the questionable honor of being eaten only at public feasts.

Because birds were small and supplied meat and eggs, they were taken along as man roamed the world. The colonists brought poultry with them to America. The Americans also had native birds, turkeys, which were introduced to Europe.

Man continued to raise poultry in much the same way as the Romans had first begun their poultry farms. The birds ran in a barnyard eating grain, scraps from the family meals, and anything else they could find. These birds were somewhat more tender and meatier than the wild ones because they didn't have to fly and hunt for food.

Few breeding improvements occurred until after World War II when great changes came about in poultry farming. The family-style barnyard operation grad-ually disappeared and was replaced by the giant, highly mechanized enterprise of to-day. Breeds were improved to produce uniform birds that were meaty and tender.

Even the function of the bird was changed. No longer were birds used for both egg laying and meat. They were developed for one or the other. No longer were chickens kept for their eggs and eaten when they were old and tough. Instead, the new breeds of chickens were ready for market in 9 weeks; turkeys, in 5 months.

Now, poultry is widely available and economical, so there can be "a chicken in every pot," as King Henry IV of France, President Herbert Hoover, and Huey Long had promised. A chicken dinner isn't just a Sunday treat, and turkey isn't only for the Thanksgiving and Christmas holidays.

Turkey-Noodle Bake

1½ cups milk
1 10½-ounce can condensed cream of mushroom soup
3 beaten eggs
3 ounces fine noodles, cooked and drained (2 cups)
2 cups cubed, cooked turkey
1 cup soft bread crumbs (1½ slices)
4 ounces sharp process American cheese, shredded (1 cup)
¼ cup chopped green pepper
¼ cup butter or margarine, melted
2 tablespoons chopped, canned pimiento

Blend milk and soup; stir in eggs. Add remaining ingredients. Turn into 11¾x7½x1¾-inch baking dish. Bake at 350° till knife inserted off-center comes out clean, 30 to 40 minutes. Cut into squares. Makes 6 to 8 servings.

Year-round barbecue

← Move barbecuing indoors when it gets cold and cook pineapple-stuffed Cornish Game Hens on a Spit on an electric rotisserie.

As an example of the growing use and popularity of poultry in menus, Americans are eating more than three times as much chicken and turkey as they did in 1940. This makes poultry third to beef and pork in per capita consumption.

Nutritional value: Poultry is an excellent nutritional meat. Just as with red meats, it supplies high-quality protein, yet poultry is often lower in calories than are the red meats. Younger birds have less fat than do the more mature birds, and geese and ducks are higher in fat than chickens and turkeys. Dark meat has slightly more calories than light meat. You can reduce the calorie count of any type of poultry by removing the skin (where the fat is stored) before cooking.

Poultry also contains iron and the B vitamins thiamine, riboflavin, and niacin. As is the case with calories, the dark meat will contain more of these important nutrients than the light meat.

How to select

Choosing the right bird for a meal and preserving its top quality is important to the consumer. Not only is this necessary for good flavor and nutrition, but it is also more economical for you.

Types of poultry: First, you must decide which type of poultry to serve—chicken, turkey, duck, goose, or guinea fowl. Chicken is readily available year-round fresh, frozen, and canned. Turkey is most often marketed frozen and is available throughout the year, too. However, during the holiday season, there is such a large demand for turkeys that it is wise to make an advance order to be assured you will have one of the desired size. Duck, goose, and guinea fowl are not readily available, but most supermarkets and meat markets do carry them at times and often will special-order them for you upon request.

Next, decide how the poultry will be cooked for this will determine the class (mature or young) that you want. If you plan on stewing or braising it, then a more mature bird will do. The slow cooking with moisture will tenderize the meat. These may be labeled mature. Mature chickens are called hen or stewing chickens. Turkeys may be labeled yearlings. If you intend to fry, broil, or roast the bird, you will want a young one. These may be labeled young, rooster, or broiler-fryer. Young turkeys are called young hen or tom; young ducks are called ducklings.

Forms of poultry: Poultry may be selected in a variety of forms—fresh, frozen, smoked, and canned. Fresh and frozen poultry is ready-to-cook. It has been completely cleaned and is ready for use.

Fresh and frozen birds are sold whole and cut into pieces. You usually save money by buying whole poultry and cutting it up yourself. There is an increase in price for the cut-up birds, but there is also an advantage of work saved and the choice of buying all pieces alike. There are also boneless roasts or rolls on the market.

Plum-Glazed Turkey Roasts

Cook turkey on the patio or with a battery-operated rotisserie at the picnic site—

 2 3- to 4-pound rolled turkey
    roasts, thawed
 1 30-ounce can purple plums
 ¼ cup frozen orange juice
    concentrate, thawed
 ½ teaspoon Worcestershire sauce
 8 to 10 drops red food coloring

Tie each turkey roast together securely with twine, if necessary. Insert a spit rod through the center of each roast; attach holding forks and test balance. Wrap turkey roasts tightly in foil, crimping the ends of the foil tightly against spit rod close to the roasts. Attach the spit to the rotisserie; roast over *medium-hot* coals for about 3 hours.

Prepare glaze by sieving the plums. Add orange concentrate, Worcestershire sauce, and food coloring. Mix the ingredients well. Bring to boiling; boil about 15 minutes. Remove foil from the roasts; brush the roasts with glaze. Insert meat thermometer. Roast till thermometer registers 185°, about 15 minutes more. Brush occasionally with glaze. Let stand 10 minutes; slice. Makes 9 to 12 servings.

Smoked poultry has a unique flavor and an added advantage of longer refrigerator storage than the fresh poultry. Canned poultry products range from whole birds to pieces of meat to prepared entrées.

Grades: When you are selecting any poultry product, the United States Department of Agriculture inspection circle and grade shield are reliable guides. These are found on all types of poultry products.

The round inspection mark reads, "Inspected for Wholesomeness by U.S.D.A." This means that the product is wholesome for food, clean, safe, accurately labeled, and not adulterated. Federal law requires that all poultry pass this federal inspection or some other equivalent inspection.

The shield-shaped grade mark is an assurance of quality. Grading is a voluntary program; therefore, poultry processors must pay for federal or federal-state grading services. Poultry can be graded only if it has passed the wholesomeness test.

The top grade for poultry is U.S. Grade A. Poultry with this stamp on it has a good overall shape and appearance, and it is meaty, full fleshed, and practically free from defects. U.S. Grade B and U.S. Grade

When making Plum-Glazed Turkey Roasts, baste rolled turkey roasts with sauce as they turn on the rotisserie over hot coals.

C poultry may have defects such as cuts and bruises and may be slightly less fleshy and meaty than the Grade A poultry.

Most of the poultry products (including whole poultry, parts, and roasts or rolls) that are found in the supermarkets are Grade A. The lower grades of poultry are usually used in processed products.

In addition to noting the grade, when buying frozen poultry, be sure that it is solidly frozen and the wrapping is not torn.

How to store

Poultry is quite perishable, so it's essential that proper care be exercised from the time of purchase till you are ready to eat it. Therefore, as soon as you arrive home, refrigerate fresh poultry or put frozen poultry into the freezer.

For short periods of refrigeration, you can leave poultry in the clear plastic wrap that the packer or market puts around it. However, if it's wrapped in market paper, unwrap it, take out the giblets, and wrap the poultry and giblets separately. It's a good idea to set the poultry on a platter to catch drippings.

If the fresh poultry won't be used within a day or two, cover it with moisture-vapor-proof wrapping and freeze it.

To use frozen poultry, cook it from the frozen state allowing extra time, or thaw it according to one of these procedures:

(1) Refrigerator thawing. Leave the original wrap on the bird and place it on a drip tray. Thaw in the refrigerator for one to three days, depending on the bird's size. When the bird is thawed, cook immediately or keep refrigerated for only a short period of time before cooking.

(2) Cold-water thawing. Leave the poultry in the original wrap, or put it into a plastic bag. Place in cold, *never warm or hot* water. Change the water frequently. Allow 30 minutes to 1 hour for small birds and 6 to 8 hours for large ones.

(3) Room-temperature thawing. Leave the bird in its original wrap. Place it in a paper bag, or wrap it in two or three layers of newspaper (this will keep the surface cool while the inside thaws). Thaw in a cool room away from heat. Thawing will take 6 to 8 hours for birds weighing 4 to 8

How to cut up poultry

To cut up poultry, cut skin between thighs and body. Grasping one leg in each hand, lift until hips are free from the body.

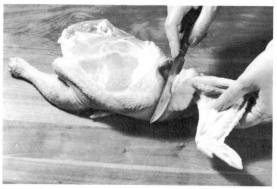

Pull the wing away from the body. Start cutting on the inside of the wing just over the joint. Cut down through the joint.

To remove the leg and thigh piece, cut between hip joint and body close to bones in back of the chicken. Repeat with other leg.

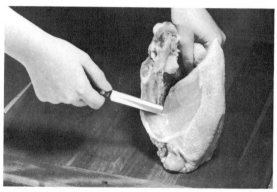

Cut along breast end of ribs to neck. Separate breast and back; cut through joints. Bend back in half to break; cut at joint.

If desired, separate the thigh and leg. Locate the knee joint by bending the thigh and leg together. Cut through this joint.

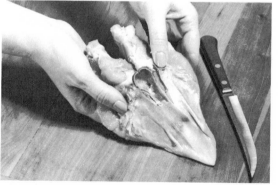

To bone breast, cut through cartilage at V of neck. Grasp small bones on each side; bend back. Push up to snap out breastbone.

pounds, and about 8 to 12 hours for those weighing between 8 and 12 pounds. Check the bird often during the last hours of thawing to prevent spoiling.

Cooked poultry must also be stored properly. Be sure to refrigerate leftovers as soon as possible. If the bird was stuffed, the stuffing *must be removed* and stored separately. Gravy should also be refrigerated separately, but if frozen, the gravy can be combined with the meat. This lengthens the storage time of the meat.

Basic preparation

Whichever method of cooking you are using for the poultry—broiling, frying, stewing, braising, or roasting—sanitary handling is important. Be sure that you clean your hands, counter top, cutting board, and knives both before and after handling. Rinse poultry with cold water and drain. Now you are ready to cook it.

Broiling: Young turkey, chicken, duck, and guinea are suitable for broiling. Small birds are split in half lengthwise or quartered, and large ones are cut into pieces. A sharp knife or poultry shears will make the job much easier. If you like, disjoint but don't separate the bones. This speeds up cooking and makes the poultry easier to handle when eating it.

Place the poultry pieces on the broiler pan or on a grill for cooking. Tuck the wings under so that they won't cook too fast. Broil with the skin side away from the heat first, then turn. Baste with melted butter, sauce, or glaze during broiling.

Poultry can also be broiled on a rotisserie over a grill or under a broiler. This is true of whole chicken, turkey, duck, and goose or large pieces of poultry.

To prepare poultry for the rotisserie, mount the whole birds or pieces on a spit following the manufacturer's instructions. Balance the spit for even rotation, and secure the birds tightly with prongs. If two birds are used, mount them with both head ends facing the center. If you have more than two birds, mount them crosswise on the spit. Tie the birds' wings and legs to the body so that they won't overcook or unbalance the spit as it turns.

Storage time for poultry		
Raw poultry	Refrigerator	Freezer
Chicken	1-2 days	12 months
Turkey, Duck, Goose	1-2 days	6 months
Giblets	1-2 days	3 months
Cooked poultry		
Slices or pieces	1-2 days	1 month
Slices or pieces in gravy	Refrigerate separately	6 months
Casseroles or creamed dishes	1-2 days	2-4 months

Island Broiled Chicken

　½ cup salad oil
　3 tablespoons lemon juice
1½ tablespoons soy sauce
　1 small clove garlic, minced
　½ teaspoon dried oregano leaves, crushed
　2 2-pound ready-to-cook broiler-fryer chickens, cut in half

Combine first 5 ingredients, ¼ teaspoon salt, and ⅛ teaspoon pepper for marinating sauce. Seal chickens and sauce in plastic bag. Marinate in refrigerator 4 to 5 hours, turning often. Drain chickens, reserving marinade.

Place, skin side down, in broiler pan (without rack). Broil the chickens 5 to 7 inches from heat till lightly browned, about 25 minutes. Brush occasionally with sauce. Turn; broil 15 to 20 minutes longer. Makes 4 servings.

Cornish Game Hens on a Spit

Rinse four 1-pound Cornish game hens; pat dry with paper toweling. Lightly salt cavities. Stuff with one 20½-ounce can pineapple chunks, drained. Truss birds and tie cavity closed. Mount crosswise on spit, alternating front-back, front-back. Do not have birds touching. Secure with extra-long holding forks. Combine 1 teaspoon salt; ½ cup butter, melted; and 2 tablespoons lemon juice. Brush some of this mixture on the birds. Place on rotisserie over *medium* coals. Broil 1 to 1¼ hours, brushing with sauce every 15 minutes. Makes 4 servings.

Turkey-Pineapple Grill

   1 13-ounce can pineapple chunks
   1/3 cup extra-hot catsup
   1/4 cup soy sauce
   3 tablespoons salad oil
   2 tablespoons vinegar
   2 tablespoons brown sugar
   2 tablespoons finely chopped onion
          . . .
   2 1/2 to 3 cups cooked boneless turkey
      roast, cut in 1/2-inch cubes

Drain pineapple, reserving 1/4 cup syrup. Combine the reserved syrup with catsup and the next 5 ingredients. Marinate turkey cubes for several hours in the mixture. Turn the cubes occasionally. Drain and reserve the marinade. Alternately thread turkey cubes and pineapple chunks on short skewers. Brush generously with marinade. Grill on hibachi till lightly browned, turning and brushing often with the marinade. Makes 16 appetizers.

Frying: This method of preparation is very popular, especially for chicken. However, other types of young poultry can be fried, too. The pieces of poultry are dipped in a batter, then in flour or crumbs before frying in shortening. An alternate method is oven-frying. The pieces are rolled in a commercial or homemade crumb mixture and then baked in a hot oven. This eliminates adding extra calories and frees you from watching closely.

Chicken Parmesan

   1 cup crushed, packaged, herb-
      seasoned stuffing mix
   2/3 cup grated Parmesan cheese
   1/4 cup snipped parsley
   1 2 1/2- or 3-pound ready-to-cook
      broiler-fryer chicken, cut up
   1/2 cup butter or margarine, melted

Combine stuffing mix, Parmesan, and parsley. Dip chicken in butter; roll in crumb mixture. Place pieces, skin side up and not touching, in a greased, shallow baking pan. Sprinkle with remaining butter and crumbs. Bake at 375°till done, about 1 hour. Do not turn. Serves 4.

Stewing and braising: These methods of cooking are similar in that both involve cooking in a liquid. With stewing, the poultry simmers in water or broth. This technique is often used for older birds. The long, slow cooking helps to tenderize and bring out the flavor of the meat.

Braising involves two steps. First, the meat is browned for an attractive appearance. Then, the poultry simmers in a small amount of broth or sauce. This helps to tenderize mature poultry, and it also imparts the flavor from the liquid into both older and younger poultry.

Spanish-Style Chicken

   1 2 1/2- to 3-pound ready-to-cook
      broiler-fryer chicken, cut up
   3 tablespoons shortening
   1/2 cup chopped onion
   1 clove garlic, minced
   1 cup tomato juice
   2 cups chicken broth
   1 cup uncooked long-grain rice
   1 10-ounce package frozen peas,
      broken apart
   1/4 cup chopped, canned pimiento

Season chicken with 1 teaspoon salt and 1/4 teaspoon pepper. In skillet brown chicken in hot shortening. Add 1/2 cup chopped onion and minced garlic; cook till onion is tender but not brown. Add tomato juice and 1/2 *cup* chicken broth. Cover; simmer for about 20 minutes.

Add rice and remaining broth. Simmer, covered, for 20 minutes. Add peas and pimiento. Simmer till peas are tender, about 5 minutes longer, stirring once or twice. Makes 4 servings.

Roasting: Roasting is one of the most popular ways to cook poultry. This method leaves the bird in an attractive shape and able to hold a stuffing.

With a Spanish flair

Set the theme for a foreign menu with →
Spanish-Style Chicken and avocado halves. Then, add bread sticks and a crisp salad.

Poultry roasting chart

General Roasting: Stuff, if desired. Truss. Place, breast side up, on rack in shallow roasting pan. Rub skin with salad oil. If meat thermometer is used, insert without touching bone in center of inside thigh muscle. Roast, uncovered, according to chart. When bird is $\frac{2}{3}$ done, cut band of skin or string between legs and tail. Continue roasting till done.

Test for Doneness: The thickest part of the drumstick should feel very soft when pressed between fingers protected with paper towels. The drumstick should move up and down and twists easily in socket. Meat thermometer should register 185°. Remove bird from oven; let stand 15 minutes so that meat can firm up before carving. (See Carving.)

Poultry	Ready-To-Cook Weight	Oven Temp.	Roasting Time Stuffed and Unstuffed	Special Instructions
Chicken	1½-2 pounds	375°	¾-1 hr.	Brush dry areas of skin occasionally with pan drippings. Cover loosely with foil.
	2-2½ pounds	375°	1-1¼ hrs.	
	2½-3 pounds	375°	1¼-1½ hrs.	
	3-4 pounds	375°	1½-2 hrs.	
	4-5 pounds	375°	2-2½ hrs.	
Capon	4-7 pounds	375°	1½-2 hrs.	Same as above.
Turkey	6-8 pounds	325°	3½-4 hrs.	Top loosely with foil. Press lightly at end of drumsticks and neck, leaving air space between bird and foil. Last 45 minutes, cut band between legs and tail; continue roasting, uncovering, till done.
	8-12 pounds	325°	4-4½ hrs.	
	12-16 pounds	325°	4½-5½ hrs.	
	16-20 pounds	325°	5½-6½ hrs.	
	20-24 pounds	325°	6½-7½ hrs.	
Foil-wrapped Turkey	8-10 pounds	450°	2¼-2½ hrs.	Place trussed turkey, breast up, in center of greased, wide heavy foil. Bring ends of foil up over breast; overlap fold and press up against ends of turkey. Place bird in shallow pan (no rack). Open foil last 20 minutes to brown turkey.
	10-12 pounds	450°	2½-3 hrs.	
	14-16 pounds	450°	3-3¼ hrs.	
	18-20 pounds	450°	3¼-3½ hrs.	
	22-24 pounds	450°	3½-3¾ hrs.	
Domestic Duck	3-5 pounds	375° then 425°	1½-2 hrs. 15 minutes	Prick skin well all over to allow fat to escape. Do not rub with oil.
Domestic Goose	4-6 pounds	325°	2¾-3 hrs.	Prick legs and wings with fork so fat will escape. During roasting, spoon off fat in pan. Do not rub with oil.
	6-8 pounds	325°	3-3½ hrs.	
	8-10 pounds	325°	3½-3¾ hrs.	
	10-12 pounds	325°	3¾-4¼ hrs.	
	12-14 pounds	325°	4¼-4¾ hrs.	
Cornish Game Hen	1-1½ pounds	375°	1½ hrs.	Roast, loosely covered, for 30 minutes, then 60 minutes uncovered or till done. If desired, occasionally baste with melted butter or glaze the last hour.
Guinea Hen	1½-2 pounds	375°	¾-1 hr.	Lay bacon over breast. Roast loosely covered. Uncover last 20 minutes.
	2-2½ pounds	375°	1-1½ hrs.	

To prepare the bird for roasting, rinse and drain it. Then, rub the inside with salt, if desired. The salt is usually omitted if a stuffing is to be added. If you are preparing a stuffed bird, mix the stuffing but *do not stuff the poultry until just before cooking.* Put some stuffing loosely into the wishbone cavity. You probably won't be able to do this on a duck or goose because of the small opening. Pull the neck skin to the back and fasten with a skewer. Then, spoon stuffing into the tail cavity, being careful not to pack it because the stuffing will expand during cooking.

The next step is to push the drumsticks under the piece of skin or a wire clamp, if provided, across the tail. If there is no band, close the opening by using wooden picks or skewers to hold the sides together. Lace the cavity shut and tie the drumsticks to the tail. Tuck the wings behind the shoulders and tie them, if necessary.

Secure the drumsticks and wings of the poultry. This keeps the bird in an attractive shape. If you desire, fill the cavity with celery and quartered onions. Discard these vegetables before serving, or save them for use in soup or gravy.

Cook the bird on a rack, breast side up, in a shallow baking pan. Rub chickens and turkeys with salad oil and baste with butter, margarine, or drippings. Cover loosely with a tent of foil, or cover the breast with a foil tent or a piece of cheesecloth that has been dipped in butter.

Ducks, geese, and guinea fowl do not require basting. Geese and large ducks have more fat than other poultry. Therefore, they are pricked before cooking around the breast, tail, wings, legs, and back so that the fat drains away.

Always cook poultry completely at one time. Never cook it partially, store it, and finish cooking it later. Partial cooking of poultry very often promotes the growth of food poisoning bacteria.

Fruit-Stuffed Goose

Make stuffing by tossing together 3½ cups soft bread cubes (4 slices); 1½ cups diced peeled apple; ½ cup chopped onion; ½ cup raisins; ½ cup melted butter; ¾ teaspoon salt; ¼ teaspoon rubbed sage; ¼ teaspoon dried rosemary leaves, crushed; and ⅛ teaspoon pepper. Stuff goose with fruit mixture. Truss the goose.

Place goose, breast side up, on rack in shallow roasting pan. Prick the legs and the wings of one 4- to 6-pound ready-to-cook goose with a fork. Roast, uncovered, at 325° for 2¾ to 3 hours, spooning off fat occasionally during cooking. Makes 4 servings.

Roast Duckling with Cranberry Sauce

Place one 3½- to 5-pound ready-to-cook duckling, breast up, on rack in shallow pan. Roast, uncovered, at 375° for 1½ hours, then at 425° till tender, 15 minutes. Place neck and giblets in saucepan. Add one 10½-ounce can condensed beef broth. Simmer, covered, for 1 hour. Strain.

To strained broth, add ¾ cup cranberry juice cocktail; cook till reduced to 1 cup. In saucepan melt 2 tablespoons butter or margarine; blend in 2 tablespoons sugar. Cook and stir till brown. Add 2 tablespoons vinegar and cranberry mixture. Remove duckling from pan. Skim fat from meat juices; add juices to cranberry mixture. Stir in 1 tablespoon cornstarch blended with 1 tablespoon cranberry juice cocktail. Cook and stir till bubbly; simmer 1 to 2 minutes. Serve giblets with the duckling and pass cranberry sauce. Makes 4 servings.

Lace cord or twine across skewers like on a boot to truss a stuffed bird. Prick the fat areas deeply, and duck is ready to roast.

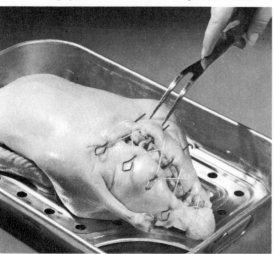

Substitute chicken for turkey sometimes to vary Swiss Turkey-Ham Bake. Either way, an artichoke-grapefruit salad, hot poppy seed rolls, and cherry parfaits complement the main dish.

Roasting or stewing poultry has a double advantage. After the whole bird appears as a main course, the leftovers can be used in casseroles, soups, salads, and sandwiches. This saves the homemaker time, and it disguises the food so the family doesn't become bored with repetition.

Turkey-Crab Sauce

Prepare rich biscuit dough or puff pastry shells. *Or* halve and seed 3 medium acorn squash; cook till tender. Dot with butter.

In saucepan combine 2 cups dairy sour cream; one 7½-ounce can crab meat, drained, flaked, and cartilage removed; 2 cups diced, cooked turkey *or* chicken; and 2 tablespoons sauterne. Place the mixture over low heat just till serving temperature. Spoon mixture over biscuits, puff pastry shells, or squash halves. Sprinkle ¼ cup shredded process Swiss cheese over top. Serve at once. Makes 6 servings.

Swiss Turkey-Ham Bake

Convert leftovers into an elegant dish by adding water chestnuts, wine, and cheese—

In skillet cook ½ cup chopped onion in 2 tablespoons butter or margarine till onion is tender but not brown. Blend in 3 tablespoons all-purpose flour, ½ teaspoon salt, and ¼ teaspoon pepper. Add one 3-ounce can sliced mushrooms, undrained, 1 cup light cream, and 2 tablespoons dry sherry; cook and stir till the mixture is thickened and bubbly.

Add 2 cups cubed cooked turkey, 1 cup cubed, fully cooked ham, and one 5-ounce can water chestnuts, drained and sliced.

Pour into a 1½-quart casserole; top with 2 ounces process Swiss cheese, shredded (½ cup). Mix 1½ cups soft bread crumbs and 3 tablespoons butter or margarine, melted; sprinkle bread crumb mixture around edge of casserole. Bake at 400° till lightly browned, about 25 minutes. Makes 6 servings.

POULTRY SEASONING—A commercial mixture of ground herbs and spices used primarily to season poultry stuffings and poultry dishes. A typical blend includes thyme, sage, pepper, marjoram, and nutmeg. Savory, ginger, allspice, cloves, and mace may also be used.

Its use is not limited to poultry stuffings, casseroles, and giblet gravies. Poultry seasoning also highlights the flavor of stuffings for veal, pork, and fish and accents meat loaves, biscuits, gravies, and dumplings. (See also *Herb.*)

Chicken à la France

      ¼ cup all-purpose flour
      ½ teaspoon salt
        Dash pepper
      1 2½- to 3-pound ready-to-cook
          broiler-fryer chicken, cut up
      2 tablespoons chopped onion
      2 tablespoons butter or margarine
              • • •
      1 11-ounce can condensed Cheddar
          cheese soup
      ½ cup canned tomatoes
      ¼ cup sauterne
      ¼ teaspoon poultry seasoning
      ⅛ teaspoon garlic powder

Combine flour, salt, and pepper in paper or plastic bag; add 2 or 3 pieces chicken at a time; shake to coat. Brown chicken and onion in butter in a skillet.

Combine soup and remaining ingredients. Blend well. Pour over browned chicken. Cook, covered, over low heat till chicken is tender, about 40 minutes; stir often. Serves 4.

POULTRY SHEARS—A heavy-duty instrument that resembles scissors or wire clippers. Poultry shears are especially useful in the kitchen for cutting through the flesh and bones of all types of poultry.

POUND CAKE—A rich, moist, compact cake that is usually baked in a loaf. Pound cake was once made with a pound each of butter, sugar, eggs, and flour; hence, the name pound cake. This scrumptious dessert cake now has different proportions and includes baking powder as a leavening agent. Lemon or spices are sometimes included to enhance the flavor of the cake.

Never before has it been easier to make pound cake than it is today. You can make the cake from basic ingredients, using tested recipes, or from cake mixes. If you decide not to make the cakes yourself, good packaged bakery cakes and frozen ones are available in the supermarkets.

There are a few techniques to follow when making your own pound cake. First, have all the ingredients at room temperature before you begin. Then, be sure to beat the batter sufficiently—this is the key to a good pound cake. Always follow the recipe directions or package instructions for length of beating time, especially for beating the batter thoroughly after adding each egg. Today, with the aid of electric mixers, it is much easier and quicker to beat batters than it was in years past when homemakers spent as long as an hour beating cake batters by hand.

Swirl chocolate- and lemon-flavored batters together for the marbled effect found in the flavor and color of Marble Pound Cake.

Freshly baked pound cake makes a delicious dessert by itself, or with butter or a fruit sauce. The cake has other uses, too. Cubes or fingers are excellent topped with a pudding or arranged around the edges of a bowl before adding a creamy filling. The slices substitute for bread when making party or tea sandwiches. If the cake becomes stale, it can be salvaged by toasting or soaking in wine.

Pound cake that is not used immediately will store well. It should be wrapped tightly. The cake will keep well in the refrigerator or in the freezer for as long as six months. (See also *Cake*.)

Marble Pound Cake

    1¼ cups sugar
    ¾ cup butter or margarine,
        softened
    ½ cup milk
    1 teaspoon grated lemon peel
    1 tablespoon lemon juice
    2¼ cups sifted cake flour
    1¼ teaspoons salt
    1 teaspoon baking powder
    3 eggs
            • • •
    2 tablespoons boiling water
    1 tablespoon sugar
    1 1-ounce square unsweetened
        chocolate, melted
        Confectioners' sugar

In large mixer bowl gradually beat the 1¼ cups sugar into the butter or margarine. Cream till light and fluffy, 8 to 10 minutes at medium speed on electric mixer. Beat in milk, lemon peel, and juice. Sift together flour, salt, and baking powder. Add to creamed mixture and mix on low speed till smooth, about 2 minutes. Add eggs, one at a time, beating 1 minute after each; beat for 1 minute more, scraping sides of bowl often. Combine the boiling water, the 1 tablespoon sugar, and the melted chocolate; stir into *half* the batter. In greased 9x5x3-inch loaf pan, alternate light and dark batters by spoonfuls. With narrow spatula, gently stir through batter to marble. Bake at 300° about 1 hour and 20 minutes. Cool 10 minutes before removing from pan. When completely cool, sift confectioners' sugar over top of cake.

Loaf Pound Cake

    ¾ cup butter or margarine
    ½ teaspoon grated lemon peel
    ¾ cup sugar
    1 teaspoon vanilla
    3 eggs
    1¼ cups sifted all-purpose flour
    ½ teaspoon baking powder

Cream butter and lemon peel; gradually add sugar, creaming till light, about 6 minutes at medium speed on electric mixer. Add vanilla, then eggs, one at a time, beating well after each. Sift together flour, baking powder, and ¼ teaspoon salt; stir in. Grease *bottom* only of 9x5x3-inch pan; turn in batter. Bake at 350° till done, about 50 minutes. Cool in pan. Sift confectioners' sugar on top, if desired.

POUSSE CAFÉ (*poos' ka fa'*)— **1.** Any liqueur served in a cordial glass with coffee after dinner. **2.** An after-dinner drink made by layering from two to seven liqueurs of different colors, flavors, and densities in a cordial glass. This rainbow-colored drink is spectacular and impressive.

Experimentation with various combinations and brands of liqueurs is necessary to perfect your technique in making a pousse café. Start with a narrow cordial glass and from two to seven liqueurs. To keep the layers separate, you must put the heaviest liqueur on the bottom and graduate up to the lightest on the top. A typical combination includes, from bottom to top, green crème de menthe, yellow chartreuse, cherry-flavored liqueur, and cognac.

Layering the liqueurs in the glass requires a steady hand. Use one teaspoon to one tablespoon of each liqueur, depending on the number of layers. Pour each layer gently down the side of the glass or over the back of a demitasse spoon that is placed in the glass upside down.

POWDERED SUGAR—Term for confectioners' sugar. (See also *Confectioners' Sugar*.)

PRALINE (*pra' len, pra' lin, pra len'*)—A rich, creamy, patty-shaped candy. Pralines are usually made with granulated sugar, brown sugar, corn syrup, milk or cream, butter, and pecans. However, this is not the way the original pralines were made. The first ones were delicious sugar-coated almond confections made by the French chef of Marshal César du Plessis Praslin. The name, praline, is said to have been derived from the marshal's last name.

Pralines were brought to America by New Orleans travelers who visited France. The renowned Creole cooks adapted the recipe by adding brown sugar and changing the nuts to pecans. Since that time, New Orleans and the South have become quite famous for their smooth praline candies and praline-flavored toppings for desserts and as after-dinner confections.

Homemakers who want to make these nutty, rich candies can do so easily. Simply follow the recipe directions carefully and use the basic principles of making crystalline candy. (See also *Candy*.)

Creamy Pralines

        2 cups sugar
      ¾ teaspoon baking soda
        1 cup light cream
            •   •   •
    1½ tablespoons butter or margarine
        2 cups pecan halves

Combine sugar and baking soda in 3½-quart saucepan; mix well. Stir in cream. Bring to boiling over medium heat, stirring constantly. Reduce heat; cook and stir to soft-ball stage (234°). (Mixture caramelizes slightly.) Remove mixture from heat; add butter. Stir in pecan halves; beat till thick, about 2 to 3 minutes. Drop from tablespoon onto waxed paper-lined cookie sheet. If candy becomes too stiff, add a tablespoon hot water. Makes 30 pralines.

Pralines

            Butter or margarine
    1½ cups brown sugar
    1½ cups granulated sugar
        3 tablespoons dark corn syrup
        1 cup milk
            •   •   •
        1 teaspoon vanilla
    1½ cups pecan halves

Butter the sides of a heavy 3-quart saucepan. In it combine brown sugar, granulated sugar, dark corn syrup, and milk. Cook and stir over medium heat till the sugars dissolve and the mixture boils. Cook to soft-ball stage (234°), stirring occasionally. Cool 10 minutes.

Add vanilla to the candy mixture. Beat by hand 2 minutes. Add pecan halves; beat till the mixture loses its gloss. Drop by tablespoons onto waxed paper-lined cookie sheet. If candy becomes too stiff to drop, add a teaspoon of hot water. Makes 16 pralines.

PRAWN—A shellfish similar to the shrimp. Prawns, like shrimp, inhabit fresh and saltwaters in tropical and temperate regions. These two shellfish look alike, causing them to be confused in markets and on menus. Prawns, however, grow to a larger size than does the average shrimp.

Prawns are considered a great delicacy, especially by the Europeans who eat them more than Americans do.

Clean, cook, and serve prawns in the same way as large shrimp. (See *Shellfish, Shrimp* for additional information.)

Boiled Prawns

        6 quarts water
        1 tablespoon salt
    1½ pounds frozen raw prawns,
            in the shell
            Cocktail Sauce (See *Cocktail*)

In large kettle bring water and salt to boiling. Add frozen prawns. Return to boiling; reduce heat and boil gently for 2 minutes. Drain the prawns. Cool quickly in cold water. Peel and devein prawns. Serve with Cocktail Sauce, if desired. Makes 3 or 4 servings.

PRECOOK—To completely or partially cook a food before it's used as an ingredient in a recipe. Vegetables are often precooked. For instance, whole green peppers are boiled a few minutes before being stuffed with a meat mixture so that the peppers will be tender. Variety meats are precooked by simmering in water for 30 minutes. This improves the texture and flavor.

Commercial products are sometimes precooked for faster preparation at home. One of the most common is packaged precooked rice. You can prepare this type of rice in very little time.

PREHEAT—To bring an oven or a cooking utensil to the desired temperature before putting the food into it. Preheating is necessary to start cooking immediately and to produce uniform cooking results.

Ovens should always be preheated unless the recipe specifically directs you to begin in a cold oven. About 10 minutes are needed for most ovens to preheat. Many ovens have a signal light to show when the oven has reached the preset temperature.

Broilers are not always preheated. The manufacturer's instructions will tell you whether to preheat or not. Skillets, waffle bakers, and griddles are preheated. This sears meats, cooks foods quickly with little loss of flavor and nutrition, and prevents overcooking of the foods.

PREPARED HORSERADISH—A condiment containing ground horseradish root and white vinegar. Bottles of prepared horseradish are found in supermarket refrigerator cases. Keep it refrigerated at home to preserve flavor and quality.

Prepared horseradish loses its strength gradually. Therefore, older bottles of horseradish will not give as much hot flavor or bite as newer bottles of it will. You can compensate for this by adding a little more than usual until the flavor suits your taste. (See also *Horseradish*.)

PREPARED MUSTARD—A bright yellow condiment prepared from dry, ground mustard seeds. The dry mustard is usually mixed with wine or vinegar, but sometimes water or beer is used. Various spices and seasonings are also added by manufacturers to give a distinctive taste. Dijon-style and horseradish mustard are examples of specially flavored mustards.

Prepared mustard is one of America's favorite condiments. It's a must on hot dogs and many other sandwiches. It lends zesty flavor and color when used as an ingredient in salads, appetizers, sauces, and main dishes. (See also *Mustard*.)

Ham Salad Supreme

    2 3-ounce packages lemon-flavored gelatin
  ½ cup dairy sour cream
1½ teaspoons prepared horseradish
1½ teaspoons prepared mustard
  ¼ teaspoon salt
  2 3-ounce packages smoked sliced ham, snipped
  ½ cup diced celery

Dissolve gelatin in 2 cups boiling water. Stir in 1 cup cold water. To ½ *cup* gelatin, add sour cream, prepared horseradish, prepared mustard, and salt. Beat mixture just till smooth with rotary beater. Pour into 5½-cup mold. Chill the mixture till it is *almost* firm.

Meanwhile, chill remaining gelatin till partially set. Fold in ham and celery. Carefully pour over almost firm sour cream layer. Chill till firm. Makes 5 servings.

Franks in Foil

  2 cups finely chopped frankfurters
⅓ cup shredded sharp process American cheese
  2 hard-cooked eggs, chopped
  3 tablespoons chili sauce
  2 tablespoons pickle relish
  1 teaspoon prepared mustard
¼ teaspoon celery seed
  8 frankfurter buns, split

Combine all ingredients *except* buns. Fill buns with frankfurter mixture. Wrap each securely in foil. Place on baking sheet; bake at 400° for 15 to 18 minutes. Makes 8 sandwiches.

PRESERVATIVE—A natural or chemical substance that keeps foods from spoiling. Salt, sugar, wood smoke, spices, vinegar, alcohol, and brine have been used for centuries to preserve foods. For instance, ham is preserved with wood smoke, and anchovies are packed in a brine.

More recently, chemical compounds have been added to foods to lengthen storage time, retain flavor, and postpone fermentation or decomposition. Salad oil and shortening do not become rancid as fast as they used to because of antioxidants, and breads do not mold rapidly because of the sodium and calcium propionate added.

The additives that are used in foods are approved by the Food and Drug Administration. (See also *Food Additive*.)

PRESERVE—1. Whole fruit or large pieces of fruit in a thick syrup. **2.** To prepare foods, usually by canning or freezing, so that they will keep for later use.

Preserves are usually made with acid fruits such as peaches, pears, pineapple, raspberries, cherries, and strawberries. The fruit is cooked in sugar and water until it's tender, clear, and a bright, good color. The fruit should hold its shape and dominate the flavor of the sugar. Besides adding sweetness and acting as a preservative, the sugar syrup also penetrates and plumps the fruit.

Hot preserves are packed into hot jars and sealed. These jars store well in a cool, dark, dry place. Once the jars are opened, they should be refrigerated.

Preserves are delicious as snack spreads on breads or muffins. They are tasty and attractive served as accompaniments in a meal. Preserves also add flavor and color when used as ingredients in desserts, breads, and glazes for meats.

Winter Preserves

  1½ cups prunes
  1½ cups dried apricots
   1 large orange
   1 8¾-ounce can crushed pineapple
   5 cups sugar

Rinse prunes and apricots. Cover with 5 cups water in medium saucepan. Simmer, covered, 15 minutes; drain, reserving liquid. Cool. Pit and cut up prunes. Cut up apricots. Peel orange, reserving peel. Section orange, saving juice. Dice orange sections. Scrape; discard white portion. Slice peel into *thin* slivers.

In large kettle combine prunes, apricots, reserved cooking liquid, orange peel, orange sections and juice, *undrained* pineapple, and sugar. Boil gently till desired thickness, about 20 minutes, stirring occasionally. Seal in hot, scalded jars. Makes three ½ pints.

Pineapple Drop Cookies

  ¾ cup butter or margarine,
     softened
   1 cup sugar
   1 egg
  ¼ cup pineapple preserves
  2½ cups sifted all-purpose flour
   1 teaspoon baking soda
  ½ teaspoon salt

Cream butter or margarine and sugar till light. Beat in egg and pineapple preserves. Sift together dry ingredients; add to batter, mixing thoroughly. Drop from teaspoon, 2 inches apart, on *ungreased* cookie sheet. Bake at 375° for 10 minutes. Cool 1 or 2 minutes; remove from pan. Top with preserves and a walnut half just before serving, if desired. Makes 42 cookies.

Jubilee Sauce

   1 16-ounce jar dark cherry
     preserves
  ¼ cup port
  ¼ teaspoon almond extract

Combine dark cherry preserves, wine, and almond extract; chill. Serve sauce over ice cream or filled cream puffs. Makes 1⅔ cups.

Plum-Glazed Ribs

   4 pounds pork loin back ribs, cut
     in serving-sized pieces
   1 10-ounce jar plum preserves
  ¼ cup frozen orange juice
     concentrate, thawed
   1 tablespoon vinegar
  ½ teaspoon Worcestershire sauce

Place ribs, meaty side down, in shallow roasting pan. Roast at 450° for 30 minutes. Remove meat from oven; drain off excess fat. Turn ribs meaty side up; season with 2 teaspoons salt. Reduce oven temperature to 350° and continue roasting for 1 hour; drain.

Meanwhile prepare plum glaze by combining preserves, orange juice concentrate, vinegar, and Worcestershire sauce; blend. Pour glaze over ribs; roast till tender, 30 minutes, basting occasionally. Makes 4 to 6 servings.

Cherry-Sauced Pork Loin

Excellent for holiday dinners—

  1 4- to 5-pound pork loin roast,
      boned, rolled, and tied
½ teaspoon salt
½ teaspoon pepper
   Dash dried thyme leaves,
   crushed
  1 cup cherry preserves
¼ cup red wine vinegar
  2 tablespoons light corn syrup
¼ teaspoon ground cinnamon
¼ teaspoon ground nutmeg
¼ teaspoon ground cloves
¼ teaspoon salt
¼ cup toasted, slivered almonds

Rub roast with a mixture of the ½ teaspoon salt, pepper, and thyme. Place the roast on rack in a 13x9x2-inch baking pan. Roast, uncovered, at 325° for about 2½ hours.

Meanwhile make cherry sauce in small saucepan by combining cherry preserves, vinegar, corn syrup, cinnamon, nutmeg, cloves, and the ¼ teaspoon salt. Heat to boiling, stirring occasionally; reduce heat and simmer 2 minutes more. Add the toasted, slivered almonds.

Spoon sauce over roast and continue roasting till meat thermometer registers 170°, about 30 minutes longer. Baste roast with cherry sauce several times. Pass sauce with the roast. Makes 10 to 12 servings.

Glazed Pork Shoulder

Glaze adds flavor plus color—

  1 4- to 6-pound fresh pork
      shoulder roast
      • • •
½ cup apricot preserves
  2 teaspoons vinegar
  1 teaspoon prepared mustard
¼ teaspoon ground ginger

Place meat on rack in shallow roasting pan. Roast at 325° till the meat thermometer registers 185°, about 4 hours. Combine preserves, vinegar, mustard, and ginger. Remove meat from the oven; spoon on sauce. Roast 15 minutes more. Makes 12 to 16 servings.

Apricot-Ham Patties

1½ pounds ground fully cooked ham
½ cup soft bread crumbs
½ cup milk
  2 eggs
¼ cup chopped onion
  1 ounce blue cheese, crumbled
    (¼ cup)
  1 tablespoon Worcestershire sauce
  1 teaspoon prepared mustard
¼ teaspoon ground sage
¼ teaspoon pepper
      • • •
½ cup apricot *or* peach preserves
  2 teaspoons vinegar
  1 teaspoon prepared mustard

Combine ham, bread crumbs, milk, eggs, onion, cheese, Worcestershire sauce, mustard, sage, and pepper. Shape in 6 patties. Place in a 13x9x2-inch baking dish; bake at 350° for 30 minutes. Combine preserves, vinegar, and mustard; brush mixture on the ham patties. Bake 10 minutes longer. Makes 6 servings.

Foods that are preserved for later use include fruits, vegetables, and meats. These have been preserved in various ways since the beginning of civilization. Methods used for preserving foods include drying, smoking, curing, canning, freezing, pickling, and jelly- or jam-making. The newest methods are dehydrating and freeze-drying. (See *Canning, Freezing, Jelly* for additional information.)

PRESERVED GINGER—Fresh ginger packed in a heavy syrup. Bottles of preserved ginger consist of cleaned, peeled, and boiled ginger preserved in a sugar solution. Preserved ginger is used as a sauce or an ingredient. This ginger comes from Hong Kong and Australia. (See also *Ginger*.)

PRESSED COOKIE—A rich cookie shaped by forcing the dough through a cookie press. Spritz are one of the better-known pressed cookies. These cookies make attractive gifts and party refreshments because of their shapes. Tint the dough to add a seasonal color. (See *Cookie, Spritz* for additional information.)

PRESSED DUCK—A dish consisting of sliced duck meat and a sauce made with the juices extracted from the duck carcass.

This delectable French dish is traditionally prepared at the dinner table. When the whole, roasted duck is brought to the table, the legs are removed and the breast meat is sliced. Then, the remaining duck is put into a duck press (usually an ornate piece of equipment). The juices are pressed out, cooked down, and blended with wine and brandy to make the sauce that garnishes the sliced breast meat.

PRESSURE COOKING—A method of cooking foods with pressurized steam using a specially designed pan. One of the main advantages of pressure cooking is speed, especially in high-altitude areas. In fact, pressure pans were once known as Denver cookers because they were so widely used around that area of the country.

The basic principle of pressure cooking is that steam is held in the pan under pressure so that the temperature is higher than the boiling point of water. Therefore, foods cook in about a third of the time required by normal methods. Because of the short cooking time and the small amount of water used in pressure cooking, the vitamins and minerals in food and the bright color of vegetables are preserved. Pressure cooking helps to tenderize the less-tender cuts of meat such as stewing meats, pot roasts, and older poultry.

Equipment: The pressure pan consists of several basic parts—the pan, cover, sealing gasket, pressure indicator, and safety valve or automatic air vent.

The pans are constructed of sheet or cast aluminum or of stainless steel. Saucepans come in sizes of 4, 6, and 8 quarts. The canners are larger than saucepans and range up to 21-quart capacities.

The covers are constructed so they lock tightly onto the pan. The gasket, usually rubber, helps to seal the two together. The pressure indicator shows how many pounds of pressure are inside the pan.

Air vents and safety valves in the covers are made of metal or rubber. Both types are designed to release steam if pressure is not released immediately.

Guide to pressure pans

Pressure saucepan — a deep pan shaped either like a saucepan or a more shallow skillet. These have one long handle. Some models are electric and have controlled heat.

Pressure cooker or canner — A utensil larger than the saucepan.

Cookers and saucepans can be used interchangeably: canners to cook large quantities of food as well as processing canned food; and saucepans to can small jars of food.

How to care for pressure pans: Always study the instruction booklet that comes with a pan and keep it in a convenient place. The booklet will give specific instructions for your particular utensil.

Generally, pressure pans should be handled with care. Do not drop or bang them, for this can cause cracks and chips. Clean all parts after each use, being sure the vent tube is completely clean. Avoid putting any parts of the pan into water if the instructions say "not immersible."

Store all parts of the pan together. The cover should not be fastened on the pan, so turn it upside down over the pan, or store inside or separately.

How to cook in a pressure pan: Cooking in pressure pans is simple and safe if you follow the manufacturer's directions. Be sure to keep the vent clean, use the correct amount of water, and control the heat.

Follow the recipe directions for the amount of food and water to be put into the pan, filling the pan only ½ to ⅔ full. Check to see that the vent is not clogged and then fasten the cover securely. Begin heating the pan and place the pressure indicator on as the instruction specifies. When it reaches the correct pressure, begin timing and lower the heat to keep the pressure constant. You should stay near the pan to control the heat.

Remove the pan from the heat immediately when the recommended time is up to avoid overcooking. Depending on the food, pressure is completely reduced in one of two ways: (1) removing the pan from the heat and letting the pressure drop of its own accord; or (2) *cooling* the pan quickly by placing it under running, cold water, by pouring cold water over the top, or by setting the pan in cold water. To be sure the pressure is down, test by tilting the pressure indicator slightly. If there is no steam, the pressure is down and you can remove the food safely.

How to can in a pressure pan: Processing in a pressure canner is necessary when canning many types of foods. Low-acid foods such as meats and most vegetables must have a higher temperature than boiling water to kill spoiling bacteria.

To can foods in a pressure canner or cooker, follow the directions in your instruction booklet. Put the correct amount of water in the canner. Place the jars of food on a rack in the canner so that steam can flow around each jar. Lock the cover in place and heat the canner. Let the steam escape for about seven to ten minutes so the air is removed from the utensil and jars. Then, put the pressure indicator in place and bring the pan to the pressure called for. Adjust the heat to hold this pressure. Process for the length of time specified in the recipe. When the time has elapsed, remove the pressure pan from the heat and let the pressure go down by itself. When all the pressure is gone, remove the pressure indicator and then the cover. (See also *Canning*.)

Quick Ribs and Kraut

  2 pounds pork spareribs
  1 27-ounce can sauerkraut,
    undrained
½ cup tomato juice
  2 tablespoons brown sugar

Cut ribs in serving-sized pieces. In skillet brown ribs on both sides. In 4-quart pressure pan combine sauerkraut, tomato juice, and brown sugar. Top with ribs; season with salt and pepper. Close cover securely. Cook at 15 pounds pressure for 15 minutes. Cool pan by placing under cold running water. Serves 4 or 5.

Pork Chop Supper

  2 teaspoons shortening
  4 pork chops, ½ inch thick
  1 teaspoon salt
    Dash pepper
½ cup chicken broth
  4 small potatoes, peeled and halved
    or quartered
  4 medium carrots, peeled and
    cut up
  1 small onion, chopped
    Salt and pepper

      • • •

  2 tablespoons all-purpose flour
¼ cup cold water

Heat shortening in a 4-quart pressure pan. Season chops with the 1 teaspoon salt and dash pepper; brown the chops on both sides in hot shortening. Add chicken broth. Place potatoes, carrots, and onion atop chops. Sprinkle with additional salt and pepper. Close cover securely. Cook 10 minutes at 15 pounds pressure. Cool quickly under cold running water.

Remove chops and vegetables to serving platter. Blend flour and cold water. Add to juices in pan. Cook and stir till thickened and bubbly. Pass gravy. Makes 4 servings.

Jiffy Spaghetti Sauce

  2 tablespoons shortening
    or salad oil
  1 pound ground beef
  2 large onions, sliced
½ teaspoon garlic salt
  2 8-ounce cans tomato sauce
  1 6-ounce can tomato paste
  1 to 1½ teaspoons chili powder
  1 teaspoon sugar
½ teaspoon salt
    Dash cayenne

      • • •

  8 ounces long spaghetti, cooked
    Grated Parmesan cheese

Combine all ingredients *except* spaghetti and cheese in 4-quart pressure pan. Cook 12 minutes at 15 pounds pressure. Reduce the pressure quickly under cold running water. Serve sauce over hot cooked spaghetti. Top with grated Parmesan cheese. Makes 6 servings.

Saucy Chicken Dinner

    1 2½- to 3-pound ready-to-cook
        broiler-fryer chicken, cut up
    2 tablespoons shortening
    1 teaspoon salt
    ¼ teaspoon dried basil leaves,
        crushed
    1 tablespoon instant minced onion
    ½ cup chopped carrot
    1 8-ounce can tomatoes, cut up
            . . .
    1 2-ounce can chopped mushrooms,
        drained
    1 tablespoon all-purpose flour
      Hot cooked noodles

Sprinkle chicken with salt and pepper. Heat shortening in skillet. Brown chicken; place on rack in a 4-quart pressure pan. Add 1 teaspoon salt, dash pepper, basil, onion, carrot, and tomatoes with juice. Close cover securely. Cook 13 minutes at 15 pounds pressure.

Cool pan at once by placing under cold running water. Add mushrooms to saucepan; heat in open pan about 1 minute. Remove chicken to platter. Mix flour and 2 tablespoons cold water. Stir into liquid in pan and cook till thickened and bubbly. Serve over chicken and hot cooked noodles. Makes 4 servings.

PRETZEL—A crisp, biscuitlike snack shaped in a knot, stick, or circle. Originally, they were soft with a tough, chewy texture. Now, the majority are dry and hard with shiny crusts. Either type comes unsalted or studded with crystals of coarse salt.

Monks created pretzels more than fifteen hundred years ago. They were the architects of the traditional pretzel shape—a loose knot with the ends twisted in the center. Legend says that this shape was suggestive of arms crossed in prayer; therefore, priests gave pretzels to children as a reward for learning prayers.

Pretzels are now a popular snack food. They make a delicious treat eaten alone or combined with various other foods. Crisp, salty pretzels are a traditional combination with cold beer or cocktails. Pretzels also serve as good dunkers for dips and other foods. Some people are fond of them with peanut butter or mustard.

In combination with other foods, pretzels become the basis for scramble cereal mixes, another cocktail accompaniment. Crushed pretzels lend a crunchy texture and salty flavor when mixed into stuffings or sprinkled over casseroles as toppings.

Parmesan Nibble Mix

Store any leftover mix in airtight containers to serve later for snacks—

    6 cups round oat cereal
    3 cups pretzel sticks
    3 cups beer nuts
    ½ cup butter or margarine,
        melted
    1 envelope Parmesan salad
        dressing mix (1 tablespoon)

In a 13x9x2-inch baking pan heat cereal in 300° oven till warm, about 5 minutes. Remove from oven. Add pretzel sticks and beer nuts. Pour the melted butter or margarine over pretzel mixture; sprinkle with dry salad dressing mix. Stir well. Return pan to oven and heat 15 to 20 minutes longer. Makes 12 cups of nibble mix.

Ham-Pretzel Teasers

Eat the pretzel handle, too—

    1 3-ounce package cream cheese,
        softened
    1 cup ground fully cooked ham
    ¼ cup chopped pecans
    ¼ teaspoon Worcestershire sauce
      Several drops onion juice
      Thin pretzel sticks
    ½ cup finely snipped parsley

Blend cream cheese, ham, pecans, Worcestershire sauce, and onion juice; chill. Shape mixture into 3 dozen small balls. Chill till serving time. Insert pretzel stick into each ball. Roll sides in snipped parsley. Makes 3 dozen.

PRICKLY PEAR—A pear-shaped fruit that comes from any one of several cactus plants. The purple red flesh contains many large, hard seeds and is enclosed by a red, greenish red, or yellow skin. The fruit's shape and its spine-covered skin are the basis for its descriptive name.

Although there are over 100 species of prickly pears, only a few are used for food. The most familiar species are the Indian fig, tuna fig, and harberry fig. The first two are common in the southwestern United States; the last, in the east.

Prickly pear plants look different than other cacti. Instead of leaves, they have broad, flat stems or branches. Depending on the species, these stems are round-, oval-, cylindrical-, or club-shaped. The fruits that develop at the points where flowers have bloomed are actually swollen portions of the stems.

Prickly pears are another of the many foods indigenous to tropical America. Analysis of Mexican archaeological remains indicate that prickly pears were an important food as far back as 7000 B.C.

The Spanish explorers were the first Europeans to whom American Indians introduced prickly pears. In fact, at times prickly pears were the only food available to Cortez and his army as they marched through Mexico in 1519.

The Spanish took back samples of prickly pears to the Mediterranean countries where prickly pear cultivation was soon undertaken. The plants eventually spread throughout the world, becoming dietary mainstays in some countries, and troublesome weeds in others.

The name prickly pear aptly describes the appearance of this cactus fruit. When cut, the seed-filled, purple red flesh is exposed.

Nutritional value: A 3½-ounce portion of this fruit contains about 42 calories, most of which are contributed by carbohydrates. A fair amount of vitamin C is also available, while other vitamins and minerals are present in trace amounts.

How to select and store: Prickly pears are primarily available during fall and early winter. Ripeness is indicated by well-reddened skins. In addition, choose ones that are firm, yet not excessively hard, and that have a bright, fresh appearance. At home, prickly pears should be stored at a moderate room temperature.

How to prepare and use: The spines are usually removed from prickly pears prior to marketing. If not, singe them off, and peel the fruits before eating.

These juicy, succulent fruits, enjoyed raw or cooked, have a distinctive, mildly sweet flavor. When used in salads or desserts, prickly pears are left whole or are sliced or cut up, as desired. For dessert, use them sweetened, or serve with lemon wedges or cream. Cook prickly pears to make tasty jellies, jams, and preserves, too. (See also *Fruit.*)

PRIME—The top federal grade of beef, veal, and lamb. Meat labeled prime is juicy, tender, and flavorful. This grade will be found stamped on meat inside the familiar shield-shaped mark. (See *Meat, USDA* for additional information.)

PRIME RIB—A name sometimes given to a standing beef rib roast. "Prime" rib may or may not be graded as prime by the USDA. This cut is tender and flavorful. Allow 8 to 16 ounces of meat per person.

Prime rib is quite often advertised as the specialty of the house in restaurants. (See also *Beef.*)

PRINTANIER, PRINTANIÈRE (*pran ta nyā′-nyâr′*)—A garnish of mixed fresh vegetables. Printanier usually refers to a soup garnish, while printanière refers to a meat.

The vegetables used are young carrots, peas, turnips, green beans, onions, and cauliflower. These are scooped out in tiny balls or diced, then cooked, and buttered.

Smooth, mellow process cheese is easy to melt.

PROCESS CHEESE—A blend of one or more types of natural cheese that has a texture and flavor different from any of the original cheeses. Process cheese is made from ground natural cheese that is heated and treated with an emulsifying agent. The bacteria are killed in the processing, so no more curing takes place.

This processing yields a cheese that is easy to slice and to melt. The flavors are milder than the natural cheeses from which they are made. The calorie content and nutritional value of these cheeses are not changed much during processing. Process cheese keeps well.

Process cheeses were made in Germany and Switzerland as early as 1895. By 1914, they were introduced to America. Today, a third of the cheese made in America is process cheese. American cheese, a process Cheddar, ranks as the most popular of the processed cheeses.

Process cheeses come in many shapes and flavors. They may be purchased in loaves or slices. Some slices are individually wrapped. The flavors include spices, pimiento, fruit, nuts, meats, onion, shrimp, and smoke. (See also *Cheese.*)

Process cheese spreads come plain or flavored.

Cheese-Rice Squares

> 3 cups cooked rice
> 4 ounces sharp process American
>   cheese, shredded (1 cup)
> ½ cup snipped parsley
> ¼ cup finely chopped onion
> 1 teaspoon salt
> 3 beaten eggs
> 1½ cups milk
> 1 teaspoon Worcestershire sauce

Mix rice, cheese, parsley, onion, and salt. Combine eggs, milk, and Worcestershire; add to rice mixture and mix thoroughly. Pour into a greased 10x6x1¾-inch baking dish. Bake at 325° just till set, about 40 to 45 minutes. Cut in squares; top with your favorite creamed chicken or tuna. Makes approximately 6 to 8 servings.

Rice, Ham, and Cheese Salad

> ¾ cup uncooked long-grain rice
> 1½ cups water
> ¼ cup finely chopped onion
> 2 tablespoons soy sauce
> 1 medium clove garlic, minced
>   • • •
> 2 cups diced fully cooked ham
> ½ cup chopped celery
> ½ cup mayonnaise
>   or salad dressing
> 1 tablespoon vinegar
> ⅛ teaspoon cayenne
> 4 ounces process Swiss cheese,
>   shredded (1 cup)

In skillet cook rice over low heat till lightly browned. Add water, onion, soy sauce, and garlic; mix well. Cover; cook till rice is tender and liquid is absorbed, about 20 minutes. Add ham and celery; heat through. Stir in mayonnaise, vinegar, cayenne, and cheese. To serve, top with additional process Swiss cheese, if desired. Makes 4 to 6 servings.

PROCESS CHEESE FOOD—A cheese product made like process cheese but containing more moisture. It has less milk fat and less cheese than the process cheese but has added nonfat dry milk or whey solids, water, and an emulsifier. By legal definition, it

Process cheese foods are similar to process cheese.

must contain at least 51 percent cheese. Process cheese food is also called pasteurized process cheese food.

Process cheese food has a softer, more spreadable texture and melts quicker than process cheese. It makes a nice snack and blends easily into sauces or vegetables.

The cheese is available in slices, rolls, links, and loaves. Some have an additional fruit, vegetable, pimiento, or smoke flavor. It will store well like the process cheese. (See also *Cheese.*)

PROCESS CHEESE SPREAD—A cheese product that has more moisture and less fat than does process cheese food. The cheese spread comes in both jars and loaves, and may have other flavors added.

Process cheese spreads are soft enough to spread easily and to melt quickly. You can use the spread in recipes or spread it on crackers or celery for a quick snack or appetizer. (See also *Cheese.*)

PROFITEROLE (*pruh fit′ uh rōl′*)—Small cream puffs with a sweet or savory filling. The sweet type has an ice cream, custard, or jam filling and a chocolate sauce topping. The savory type has a meat, poultry, fish, or cheese filling.

PROOF—1. A standard indicating the amount of alcohol present in distilled liquor. **2.** To let yeast dough rise.

In liquor, half of the proof is the percent of alcohol. For example, if the liquor is 80 proof, this indicates that 40 percent of the liquor is alcohol.

The standard for proof came about many years ago, long before the process of distilling liquor and measuring alcohol were highly developed. The distiller would show "proof" of the alcohol content by burning a small amount.

The second meaning of proof is used in baking. When yeast dough has risen and been punched down, it is shaped and put into a pan. At this stage, the "rising" is called proofing. Proofing lasts until dough is double in bulk after which it is baked. (See also *Wines* and *Spirits.*)

PROSCIUTTO HAM (*prō shoo′ tō*)—A highly seasoned Italian ham that is cured by air-drying. Because of this curing process, prosciutto does not require further cooking. The dried, salted, and well-peppered meat is pressed, then sliced.

Prosciutto's most popular use is as an antipasto or appetizer served cold with melons or figs. Prosciutto also makes a delicious sandwich. (See also *Ham.*)

Prosciutto and Artichokes

Drain one can or jar of artichoke hearts packed in water or oil. Wrap a paper-thin slice of prosciutto ham around each artichoke heart. Secure with wooden picks. Serve as an appetizer.

Special processing concentrates the flavors in prosciutto ham, so slice it very thin and eat it with chilled wedges of honeydew.

PROTEIN—A group of highly complex substances that make up most body tissues and that perform various vital functions to maintain health, growth, and energy. Every living plant and animal has proteins in its physical makeup, and it needs a continuing supply to maintain life.

In order of quantity, proteins are second only to water in the composition of the human body. Their forms vary greatly from the soft, elastic material of muscles and organs to the tough material of bones and teeth. Other important members of this group are hemoglobin, which transports oxygen through the blood stream; antibodies, which fight disease; and enzymes, which trigger many body functions.

Proteins were first observed by a Dutch physician-chemist, Gerrit Jan Mulder. In 1838 he concluded that all plants and animals contain a substance essential to life. Although unable to analyze its components, he recognized the importance of this substance and named it "protein," from a Greek word meaning first place.

Since that time, research has shown that what Mulder observed was not one simple substance, but a group that includes hundreds of different proteins, each made up of amino acids. Eight amino acids are known to be essential for adults since these cannot be synthesized by the body. A ninth probably is essential for children.

Food proteins are classified into two biological groups: complete and incomplete. The animal proteins found in meat, milk, and eggs are complete or high quality because they contain all of the essential amino acids. Plant proteins are called incomplete because they either do not contain all of the essential amino acids, or they contain them in insufficient quantities.

This does not mean that incomplete food proteins are unimportant. Quite the contrary. Proteins in legumes and nuts come close to animal proteins in food value. Plant proteins are enhanced when served with foods that complement them nutritionally. For example, the protein in cereals is made useful when served with milk.

Protein requirements change with the age and condition of the individual. During childhood and adolescence, protein is needed for body building. Proteins are needed in greatest amounts for girls between ages 13 and 15 and boys between ages 16 and 19. Protein needs for women increase during pregnancy and nursing.

Eating meat and dairy products is the easiest but most expensive way to meet protein requirements. Inexpensive dry peas and beans, lentils, nuts, and peanut butter are rich nonanimal sources of protein that can be substituted for animal foods occasionally. (See also *Nutrition*.)

PROVENÇALE, À LA (*prō′ vuhn säl′, prov′ uhn-*)—A phrase that means "in the style of Provence" (a region in southern France). In food preparation, à la Provençale means that the food is cooked with a liberal amount of garlic and often with tomatoes and oil. Classic Provençale sauce is well suited for egg, fowl, vegetable, and meat dishes. (See also *French Cookery*.)

Sauce Provençale

4 tomatoes, peeled, each cut in 6 wedges, and seeded
½ teaspoon sugar
2 tablespoons butter or margarine
¼ cup chopped green onion
½ cup dry white wine
½ cup butter or margarine
3 cloves garlic, minced
2 tablespoons snipped parsley

Sprinkle tomatoes with sugar; set aside. Melt the 2 tablespoons butter. Add onion and heat through. Add wine; cook and stir till liquid is slightly reduced. Add tomatoes; heat through. Add remaining ingredients. Heat and stir just till butter melts. Season. Serves 6 to 8.

PROVOLONE CHEESE (*prō′ vuh lō′ nē*)—A semihard, mellow, smooth cheese that was first made in Italy but is now domestically produced, too. After it is salted and dried, this cow's milk cheese is usually smoked, then dipped in paraffin, or oiled.

Although this cheese is traditionally shaped like a pear, bound in rope baskets, and hung for curing, provolone is also formed into other shapes that range in weight from 1 to 200 pounds.

Provolone has a pleasant, smoked, sharp flavor.

Provolone is suitable for an appetizer or dessert cheese tray or for cooking. Italian cooks use provolone in many of their food dishes. (See also *Cheese*.)

PRUNE—A dried plum. Only certain varieties of plums, descendants of the European *Prunus domestica*, can be converted to prunes. In the fresh, fully ripe state, prunes are dark blue to purple in color, firm-fleshed, oblong or oval, and high in sugar content.

Plums have been an extremly important food to Europeans for many centuries, although they were not always used in the dried form. According to legend, Alexander the Great brought fresh prune plums to Europe from Persia in 331 B.C. However, the Hungarians were the first people

Prune-Nut Bread gets part of its moistness and chewiness from the prunes. Center butter balls on the platter of bread slices.

to learn how to dry them for year-round use. This drying technique spread to France where prunes became one of that country's most prized products.

The United States' cultivation and processing of prunes began in the 1850s when Louis Pellier, a French immigrant, had slips of the European prune plum trees shipped from France to California. He successfully grafted these slips from the Prune d'Agen or French prune onto wild American plum varieties. Since that time, California has become the largest prune-producing region in the world.

How prunes are produced: Like the grapes that are used for making wines, prune plums that are to be dried must be completely ripe when they are harvested so that the sugar content is at its peak. The prune plums are mechanically shaken from the trees, then dropped into canvas sheets and conveyed to large bins in which the fruits are transported to the processor.

Mechanical drying, a relatively new development, has replaced to a very large extent, the centuries-old sun-drying process. The washed prune plums are stacked on trays, then placed in temperature- and humidity-controlled dehydrators. A constant stream of warm air flows over the plums. In 18 hours the plums have become prunes containing 18 percent moisture.

Next, the prunes are graded and sized according to the number of prunes that are needed to make one pound. Placed in bulk containers, the prunes then can be stored under carefully controlled conditions until they are sold to distributors.

Just prior to packaging and shipping, the prunes are steam-treated. From 6 to 12 percent moisture is added to give the prunes more moistness and greater tenderness in the packaged state.

Nutritional value: Through the removal of water, the drying of prunes concentrates the energy and other nutrients found in the fresh prune plums. Fruit sugars present in prunes are a source of quick energy. Four medium, uncooked prunes yield 58 calories, while ½ cup prune juice provides 100 calories. Prunes are a good source of Vitamin A, iron, and potassium,

Ready-to-serve prunes and apricots are spruced up with cinnamon, lemon, and rum or brandy for Prune and Apricot Bowl.

yet are low in sodium. The soft bulking substance present in prunes acts as a natural regulator of the body processes.

How to select: The important point in prune selection is to determine which form concurs with your needs. Prunes come pitted and unpitted, dried and canned, puréed and diced, or as prune juice.

The most familiar form, ready-to-use prunes, are now tenderized to ensure moistness and tenderness right from the package. They may be purchased in various sizes—small or breakfast, medium, large, extra-large—and with or without pits.

Ready-to-serve prunes are cooked in liquid at the processing plant. These liquid packed fruits are sealed in cans and jars. Prune juice and puréed and diced prunes are more specialized products. Pureed and diced prunes are particularly good baby foods. They are also convenient items to purchase when recipes specify prunes prepared in these forms.

How to store: Storage techniques for prunes vary, depending on whether the package is unopened or opened. Both dried and canned prunes with containers intact are shelf stable. However, dried, uncanned prunes should be refrigerated if the weather gets excessively hot or humid. Use the fruit within six to eight months.

Opened packages of prunes require cool or refrigerated temperatures. Dried prunes should be tightly covered and stored in a cool, dry place. Cooked prunes should be covered and refrigerated.

How to prepare: The amount of pre-preparation required for prunes is determined by their ultimate use. For snacking, prunes are eaten right from the package. For cooked prunes, select the canned form or cook dried prunes as directed below.

Stewed Prunes

Rinse prunes and cover with water 1 inch above the fruit in a saucepan. Cover; simmer gently for 10 to 20 minutes. If desired, add 2 tablespoons sugar per cup uncooked prunes during the last 5 minutes of cooking.

Unless purchased in pitted or diced form, prunes used in recipes must first be pitted. If you wish to retain the shape of whole prunes, cut only one side of the prunes with kitchen shears and gently squeeze out the pits. Pitting and chopping are accomplished in one operation by snipping around the pits.

When extra-plump prunes are desired, add an equal measure of hot water or fruit juice to the prunes in a jar or bowl. Cover and let stand 24 hours. Store in refrigerator till you are ready to use them.

How to use: People who like prunes know the many types of recipes in which this fruit can be used. Served for breakfast or

---

Prune arithmetic

While prunes are cooking, they absorb enough water to double in bulk. One pound of dried prunes yields 4 cups cooked prunes with pits or 3 cups cooked, pitted prunes.

for a final meal course, stewed prunes get variation with the addition of a lemon slice, orange slice, or cinnamon stick.

Prune and Apricot Bowl

    2 16-ounce jars prunes
    1 30-ounce can whole apricots
    2 inches stick cinnamon
    3 tablespoons lemon juice
    1/4 cup rum or brandy

Drain and reserve syrups from prunes and apricots. In saucepan combine 1/2 cup prune syrup and 1/2 cup apricot syrup; add cinnamon and lemon juice. Simmer 2 to 3 minutes; add rum. Arrange fruits in bowl; pour hot syrup over. Serve warm or chilled. Serves 6 to 8.

Stuffed prunes provide interesting flavor and texture in salads. Prunes with cottage cheese is another salad favorite.

Stuffed Prune Salad

For each serving, arrange 2 orange slices on lettuce-lined plate. Stuff 2 cooked, pitted prunes with drained cream-style cottage cheese; top with walnut halves. Place atop oranges.

Nut breads, coffee cakes, pancakes, and waffles take on new dimensions with the incorporation of prunes, as do pies, cakes, whips, and cookies. (See *Dried Fruit*, *Plum* for additional information.)

Prune-Nut Bread

    1 cup dried prunes, chopped
    2 teaspoons shredded orange peel
    1 cup orange juice
    2 cups sifted all-purpose flour
    3/4 cup sugar
    3 teaspoons baking powder
    1/2 teaspoon salt
    1/2 teaspoon ground cinnamon
    2 beaten eggs
    2 tablespoons salad oil
    1/2 cup chopped walnuts

Combine prunes, orange peel, and juice; let stand 1/2 hour. Sift together dry ingredients. Combine eggs, oil, and prune mixture; add to dry ingredients, mixing well. Add nuts. Turn into greased 9x5x3-inch loaf pan. Bake at 350° for 55 minutes. Remove from pan; cool.

Prune Spice Cake

    1 cup sifted all-purpose flour
    2/3 cup sugar
    1 teaspoon baking powder
    1/4 teaspoon baking soda
    1/4 teaspoon salt
    1/4 teaspoon ground cinnamon
    1/4 teaspoon ground nutmeg
    1/4 cup shortening
    1/2 cup prune juice
    1 egg
    1/2 teaspoon vanilla
      Prune Butter Frosting

Sift together first 7 ingredients into mixer bowl. Add shortening, *half* the prune juice, and egg. Beat 2 minutes. Add remaining juice and vanilla. Beat 2 minutes. Pour into well-greased and lightly floured 8x8x2-inch baking pan. Bake at 350° for 25 to 30 minutes. Cool.

Frost with *Prune Butter Frosting:* Cream 3 tablespoons butter; gradually blend in 1 1/2 cups sifted confectioners' sugar and dash salt. Add enough prune juice for spreading.

PRUNE PLUM—A term applied to any plum variety that can be dried for prunes. Italian prune plums are the best-known type. However, they are eaten fresh more frequently than dried. (See also *Plum*.)

Spicy Oranges 'N Prunes

    12 whole cloves
     1 11-ounce can mandarin orange
          sections
     8 ounces unpitted dried prunes

Tie cloves in cheesecloth. Drain oranges, reserving syrup. In saucepan combine syrup, 1 1/2 cups water, prunes, and spice bag. Bring to boiling; cover and simmer 25 minutes. Add oranges. Chill. Remove spice bag. Serves 6.